Spider

Spider

Katarzyna and Sergiusz Michalski

REAKTION BOOKS

Published by
REAKTION BOOKS LTD
33 Great Sutton Street
London EC1V ODX, UK
www.reaktionbooks.co.uk

First published 2010

Printed and bound in China

British Library Cataloguing in Publication Data
Michalska, Katarzyna.
    1. Spiders. 2. Spiders – Folklore. 3. Spiders – Mythology.
    4. Spiders in art. 5. Spiders – Symbolic aspects.
    6. Spiders – Psychological aspects.
    I. Title II. Series III. Michalski, Sergiusz.
    595.4'4-DC22

ISBN: 978 1 86189 775 6

Contents

Introduction:
Spiders on the Wall
and Elsewhere

This book attempts to describe an animal whose importance lies primarily in the fact that it is – much more than most of the animals presented in this series – a cultural and psychological construct. The spider is at first sight a hauntingly real animal, never very far away from each inhabitant of the earth (save in the Arctic and the Antarctic), and strewn all over the world in almost 40,000 spider species and types, with some 500 new species still being discovered every year. Spiders might have appeared on earth around 200 million years ago. A sensational find on England's chalk cliff coast at Hastings, Sussex in summer 2009 brought to light a piece of amber in which a spider was encased. It has been dated by its discoverers as being around 140 million years old: a sensational discovery that was publicized all around the world.[1]

The fact that the myriad spiders on earth play an important role in the ecosphere – devouring harmful insects – is also generally appreciated. Nonetheless the negative attitude of most people towards the spider – though tinged by a sort of admiration – is conditioned by psychology and culture. But it is the spider's prime product, the web, that has served in modern times in an unrivalled way as a model for the organization of information and society. Earlier epochs did not see it that way.

Thanks to its domestic presence the spider was always known to virtually everybody. However, only a handful of aficionados, like the painter Odilon Redon, the Reverend Muffet or the eccentric 12th Duke of Bedford – who spoke in his memoirs, which contained a chapter entitled 'Spiders I Have Known', about his favourite house spider having a daily preference for the Duke's roast beef and Yorkshire pudding[2] – were able to build up something approaching a personal relationship with one of the eight-legged creatures. Needless to say, spiders sometimes played an important role in folktales and religious beliefs, but in Europe, in contrast to other animals, spiders did so without acquiring a distinct character of their own which might have led to a sort of anthropomorphization (although in West Africa and among the Native American tribes in North America the situation was a different one). As we shall however try to show in this book, the symbolic and psychological meanings of the spider have gained unexpectedly in stature during the course of the last century, in contrast to earlier symbolically significant animals like wolves, snakes or nightingales. All of these seem to have receded, if not faded, from the collective cultural imagination, from the imagination of their children and – perhaps most importantly – from their respective sets of animal comparatives. The very fact that the European Society of Arachnology annually bestows the title of a European Spider of the Year – in 2008 the title went to the so-called common house spider (*Tegenaria atrica*), in 2009 to the triangle spider (*Hyptiotes paradoxus*) – and that this information appeared on the front pages of major European journals, vividly demonstrates the spider's sudden rise to prominence.

The thousands and thousands of very different spider types do not lend themselves to a brief discussion of their biological and zoological characteristics. The astounding number of published spider books containing classificatory and practical information, intended both for the specialist and the general public, is another reason to pursue a different approach in this book. Spider types

An illustration of spiders of the genus *Neriene*, from John Blackwall's 1864 *A History of the Spiders of Great Britain and Ireland.*

169. N. livida, ♀♂. 170. N. errans, ♀♂. 171. N. clavis, ♂. 172. N. gracilis, ♀♂. 173. N. vagans, ♀♂. 174. N. dentata, ♂.
175. N. affinis, ♀♂. 176. N. Buthwaiti, ♂. 177. N. reyrans, ♀♂. 178. N. flavipes, ♀♂. 179. N. parva, ♂. 180. N. granata, ♀♂.
181. N. cornuta, ♀♂. 182. N. bituberculata, ♀♂. 183. N. apicata, ♂. 184. N. rubens, ♀♂. 186. N. nigra, ♀♂.
A N. marginata (see fig. 267 Pl. XVII.)

as such are thus not discussed in a comprehensive way but only case-wise, when relating in our discourse to some trait worth analysing or referring to.

The spectrum of the symbolic meanings of the spider is a very broad and varied one. Ovid's famous narrative in the *Metamorphoses* proposed – through the reference to the Lydian weaver Arachne – a personalized etymology of its Greek name, connecting the activity of the spider with the concept of weaving and artistic craft. The spider might thus symbolize creation, in some cases even the creation of the world. It stands for work and industriousness, but in the same breath might represent – given the frailty of the web – the mindless effort of work, and perhaps its pointlessness. Long is the list of supposed negative traits: over-ambitious projects, dexterity, cunning, ambition, ruthlessness, avarice, poisonousness. Nonetheless we also encounter positive

Diego Velázquez,
*The Weavers
(Las Hilanderas)*,
c. 1657, oil on
canvas, detail.

traits like caution, intellectualism, rationalism, self-reliance and self-sufficiency.

The legendary figure of Little Miss Muffet, daughter of an Elizabethan clergyman, shows vividly the problems and intricacies of man–spider relations. Her father believed spiders to be useful for curing various ailments, and thought that they beautified the home. In a classic case of child–parent opposition, Miss Muffet developed a rather severe case of arachnophobia, immortalized by a famous rhyme by Mother Goose.

It isn't just Miss Muffet: most people find the sight of a spider somewhat distasteful, if not disgusting. The spider seems a repugnant and ugly creature, its body and legs grossly disproportionate. What is more, the spider's cunningly murderous modus procedendi of catching its victims in its web, rendering them hors de combat and sucking the blood from them raises archetypal fears in humans that relate both to the ever-insecure position of primitive man, and to various nightmarish experiences in today's opaque, manipulative and deeply insecure society. It is not only misogynistic males that tend to associate the spider with female conceit, aggresssiveness and female dominance. This antifeminist stance is extended also to the sexual cannibalism of some spider species, for example Black Widow spiders (*Latrodectus mactans* and *L. hesperus*).

Some people exhibit a fondness for webs, but nonetheless hate the insect itself. The great anarchic French writer Alfred Jarry, creator of *Ubu Roi* and an excellent marksman, used to kill spiders in the centres of the webs with precise pistol shots, but boasted that he managed to leave the woven structures unharmed. While the spider can hardly be considered a positive Christian symbol, the dewy web as symbol of nature's transcendence is to be found on many modern Christian posters. Needless to say, the spider's web has exerted a particular fascination

since time immemorial. Spun out of the spider's 'own entrails', wonderfully ordered, subordinated to an all-knowing centre, it was and is admired as a wonder of nature, to refer once more to the *Metamorphoses*, which connected weaving and the spider's web to art and artistry. On the other hand it also was and is seen as the very epitome of frailty and transience, a usage inaugurated by poignant biblical metaphors.

In the popular view the spider is associated with venom and poisoning. Though the danger is for humans, save for some venomous exotic species, mostly imaginary, the negative psychological and symbolic potential of the spider – manifesting itself in irrational fits of arachnophobia – is a fact of life and certainly needs a closer analysis. These factors may explain the prevailing, mostly negative view epitomized in the old folk saying that with 'every spider you kill, you kill an enemy'. The spider itself, like the scorpion, may also constitute an aggressive political symbol: Serbian extremist militias in the Balkan wars of 1991–5

A North American garden spider and web.

Spider web in a domestic back garden.

The spider logo of the Spyder outdoor clothing firm.

wore badges with its image. The spider's web also stands for oppressive political control, for acts of entrapment committed by criminal and extortionary gangs and for the shadowy world of espionage.

The spider was and is an important symbol in various non-European civilizations, starting with the Ashanti founding myth proclaiming that all men are descended from a Great Spider. It occupies an important place in various Native American myths, in Buddhism and Taoism.

Into this traditional picture the nineteenth and especially the twentieth century have introduced new elements and trends. After 1945 the spider acquired a new place in popular urban mythology, psychological investigations, countless Hollywood horror films, design, the fashion industry (for example in the clothing of the American company Spyder), the giant sculptures of Louise Bourgeois and last but not least in politics, as a symbol for all-encompassing control. Arachnophobia – the fear of spiders that afflicted Miss Muffet – is now counted among the most interesting human neuroses, and the underlying psychological problems and symbolic associations are studied with ever greater intensity. Misogynists have a traditional preference for the spider-allegory in the form of the blood-sucking femme fatale; psychotherapists and their patients since Karl Abraham and Freud have referred to oppressive mother-spiders.

However it is increasingly the spider's web that acquires a role of its own. It has always been admired for its intricate filigree structure, and for the fact that it is both a way to gather sensory information and, when needed, a skilful instrument of capture and entanglement. The fact that it is spun out according to semi-abstract designs from the own body of the spider, that it can sometimes be recycled and used anew, can serve as a symbol of self-reliant and self-sufficient creativity, making it an important emblem for a particular type of intellectual endeavour.

However it is with the advent of modern communication technology, symbolized by the fact that the antennae of many of the early radios produced in the 1920s were given – we might say prophetically – the shape of the spider's web, that the web gained an unparalleled significance. The Ancient Greeks saw in the web an analogue of the nervous system; nowadays the myriad users of the World Wide Web and of the internet very often make use of images of the spider's web. Some of them fancy one centrally poised spider of a somewhat vague, God-like or – to put it more precisely – semi-demiurgic status; most, however, refer to themselves as spiders participating in the weaving of an all-

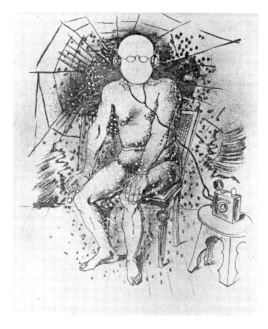

Kurt Weinhold,
The Radio Listener,
1928, drawing.

encompassing web. This latter metaphoric comparison was strengthened in 2007 by a disclaimer by Sir Tim Berners-Lee, the inventor of the World Wide Web, protesting against a comparison of the Web with the spider's web,[3] since the former has no centre (although Sir Tim does not seem to have taken into consideration the colonies of the social spider with their decentral structures). The image of the spider and its web thus represents fundamental principles of the new physical model of the world, a model derived from quantum physics: the universe is no longer a chain constituted by cause and sequence; it is – like the web – a giant network of informations and impulses transmitted in real time. The networking aspect is being stressed even in situations where ludic and jocular aims seem to predominate, for example in the public mechanical spiders in Liverpool and Yokohama. The astounding urban career of these great mechanized spiders in the years 2008 and 2009 is another proof of the astounding popularity of the spider in the end of the twentieth and the beginning of the twenty-first century.

Despite the spider's recent prominence no comprehensive history of its cultural symbolics has appeared in English or for that case in any other language; most of the concepts, themes and symbols discussed in this book have never yet received the benefit of an investigation or analysis. The impressive, though somewhat logorrheic book by the German ethnologist Bernd Rieken (*Arachne und ihre Schwestern*, 2003) occupies itself foremost with folkloric aspects and with the place of the spider in folk-beliefs and the now nascent 'urban mythology'; the two excellent German anthologies of spider literature published almost at the same time by Klaus Lindemann and Raimar Stefan Zons (1990) and by Hanne Kulessa (1991) limit themselves only to works of literary fiction and are programmatically Germanocentric. As a first attempt at a cultural synthesis submitted to an

English-speaking public, our book is no doubt saddled with omissions and might be afflicted with some outright mistakes. We have thus to ask particularly for the benevolence of all those who – like the Duke of Bedford – see in the spider something more than a noxious insect on the wall.

Tab. CCCV.

Fig. 722.

Fig. 723.

Fig. 722: Mygale fimbriata foem.
Fig. 723: M. rufidens foem.

1 Some Basic Zoological Facts

To mention a spider is, as already said, often tantamount to provoking a negative reaction. In the animal world only snakes seem to arouse a similar combination of repulsion and fear, a combination ultimately evoking mythologems of death, plague and devilish potencies. In marked contrast to snakes, spiders are an everyday phenomenon and occurrence, demanding a response from each of us, though the response is mostly a very negative one. However a closer look at our eight-legged creatures might dispel some, though certainly not all, of the many popular myths referring to their fearsome and bloodsucking traits.[1]

The large and very extended family of spiders has dwelled on earth for 350 million years. With the exception of the Arctic and the Antarctic they are to be found everywhere – in tropical forests, in deserts, high up in the mountains, in urban agglomerations and even in fresh water reservoirs. What is more, last year marine biologists found in the deep seas near Australia great 30 cm-long 'sea spiders' living at hitherto unimaginable depths of almost 3,000 metres. Discoveries can also be made nearer to home. In 2001 a new, poisonous species measuring almost 10 cm long was found in the tunnels beneath Windsor Castle. The Windsor spiders did not however seem to have disrupted the daily routine of Britain's royal family.[2]

Two Brazilian spiders: *Mygale fimbriata* (top) and *Mygale rufidens* (bottom), from C. L. Koch's 1842 *Die Arachniden.*

Tab. CCCVII.

Fig. 727. Mygale versicolor mas.

IX. 4.

Tab. CCCXIX.

Fig. 747. Mygale Javanensis mas.

IX. 6.

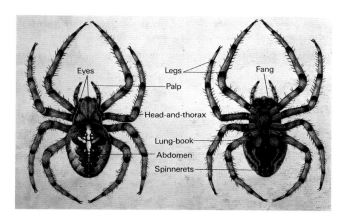

Eyes

Legs

Fang

Palp

Head-and-thorax

Lung-book

Abdomen

Spinnerets

Parts of a
spider's body.

The world is populated by a gigantic number of spiders. In some cases a meadow acre might contain over 2 million spiders, but in modern concrete and glass cities too a spider is never far away; there is usually one no more than one or two metres from us. Spiders are among nature's foremost carnivorous predators; mercilessly killing myriads of insects, they help to preserve nature's balance. When destroyed or blown away by natural catastrophes as destructive as a volcanic explosion they tend to regain control of the devastated territory very swiftly. However traditional territorial affiliations and links are now challenged by the process of globalization, massive agricultural commerce and mass tourism with spiders: for instance, poisonous Australian redback or Latrodectus spiders have travelled, hidden in imported fruit crates, to far-away places like Japan's great metropolis Osaka and have now settled there for good.

Popular opinion places spiders among the insect family. This view does not take into account some fundamental differences, since spiders lack wings and antennae and possess eight legs instead of six. In reality spiders constitute a distinct zoological

The 'Antilles pink toe tarantula' (*Mygale versicolor*, now *Avicularia versicolor*), from Koch's *Die Arachniden*.

The 'Java yellow kneed tarantula' (*Mygale javanensis*, now *Selenocosmia javanensis*), from Koch's *Die Arachniden*.

order of their own, namely the Araneae, an order which in turn belongs to the larger class of the so-called Arachnidae. This zoological class is named after the infelicitous Greek female weaver Arachne, who – according to a famous narrative of Ovid in his *Metamorphoses* – rashly challenged the Goddess Athena to a weaving contest and was in consequence transmogrified by the angry Olympian into a spider. The Araneae order includes spiders and their closest relatives: eight-legged scorpions, mites, ticks and harvestmen (also known as daddy-long-legs).

The overwhelming majority of the spider population lives in the warmer regions of the earth. As already said, in marked contrast to the six-legged insects spiders have eight limbs, their body being constituted by two so-called tagmata, the cephalothorax and the abdomen. Spinnerets protruding from the abdomen

A hunting lynx spider (*Peucetia viridans*).

extrude silk from the spider's glands. On the front and on the top of the head region we see the spider's eyes. Though some cave-dwelling species have no eyes, the great majority of the species posesses at least one and sometimes up to four pairs of eyes. Most spiders do not use their eyes for catching prey, being on the whole more active during the night, but the so-called jumping spiders and the wolf and lynx spiders hunt during the day using their eyesight. On the underside of the cephalothorax we can observe

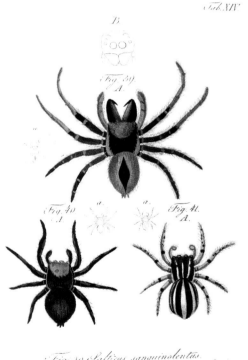

Three spiders formerly grouped together, now not: *Salticus sanguinolentus* [top; now *Philaeus chrysops*], *Salticus grossipes* [lower left; now *Evarcha arcuata*] and *Salticus fasciatus* [lower right; now *Phlegra fasciata*], from C. W. Hahn's 1831 *Die Arachniden*.

a pair of appendages and a pair of jaws. The fangs of the spider are mostly venomous, the large claws serving the purpose of capturing prey. A small mouth is positioned between the two claws.

One outstanding trait of the spider is connected with his mode of locomotion. The spider's limbs end in claws, which provide the spider with much adhesive power. The spider starts to move by raising two legs set diagonally from each other and moves on silently with great speed and alacrity. They might run swiftly for a certain distance, then suddenly stop and pretend to be asleep or dead; after that they can suddenly go in the opposite direction. We can thus never be sure as to the spider's designs or the direction he might choose. A small sensation was provided 2008 by the discovery of a new species in the Moroccan part of the Sahara, showing a hitherto unknown mode of locomotion by continually making a rolling movement with their legs, as if the legs were equipped with a kind of small wheels.[3]

A Guatemalan wolf spider.

Note the difference in size between the female *Asiope* and her diminutive mate.

Spiders can also sail through the air, covering mostly small distances but sometimes making great aerial journeys, the popular term for this ability being ballooning. In order to fly the spiders position themselves on a high point and start to emit long skeins of very light silk. Even gentle winds suffice to pull out the silk until the line is long enough to lift the spider into the air. Smaller species try on warm or windy days to use the warm air rising from the ground or to get carried by a breeze. The great majority of ballooning spiders travel only some metres, but there are situations when the spider voyages over long distances. Perhaps the first person to observe this phenomenon was Charles Darwin who, when sailing 100 kilometres away from the coast of South America in 1832, was able to see the arrival on the rigging of a great swarm of spiders. Though spiders have no influence on the direction their flight might take, they can partially determine its duration by adjusting the position of their legs and the length of the thread.

A negative factor as regards the popular reception of the spider is brought about by the mere sight of his stubbly body hair, especially that covering his legs. Though certainly less than appealing in an aesthetic or psychological sense, this hairy covering serves the spider well by aiding his faculties of recognition and perception. Endowed with nervous cells, it allows the spider to sense the slightest vibrations, to hear, feel and to taste.

The negative image of the spider is based also on a somewhat simplified view of its erotic habits. Since the females are usually much larger than the males, sometimes ten times larger (in the case of the golden orb-spider even a hundred times), they do sometimes succumb to the temptation to treat their suitors as potential victims. The supreme aim of the male during the love-play is thus to outwit his partner and so to avoid being killed during or just after the act.

The copulation and insemination takes place in a rather complicated way. Both females and males have their sexual openings beneath the abdomen. The sexually aroused male begins with the spinning of a kind of sperm web, upon which he ejaculates later on and which serves the task of transmitting his semen. During the climax of the sexual act the male injects his sperm into the female's tight genital opening. In the female spider's genitals the sperm is stored in seminal bag-like receptacles adapted to the task of preserving the semen, if necessary even for months. Many male spiders do not live to witness the moment when the female releases the sperm into herself.

The courtship and the following copulation ritual are not without picturesque moments. It begins with locating the female – since most spiders see almost nothing – through smell.

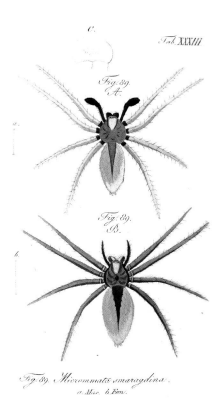

C.

Tab. XXXIII

Fig. 89. A.

a.

Fig. 89. B.

b.

Fig. 89. Micrommata smaragdina.
a. Mas. b. Fem.

The 'green huntsman spider', *Micrommata smaragdina* [now *M. virescens*], from Hahn's 1831 *Die Arachniden*.

To avoid being cast in the role of prospective victim the male often commences a refined dance, twanging and shaking the web and gesturing vivaciously. In order to curry favour with the female and deflect her attention at the same time many spider species bring her a kind of 'wedding gift'[4] – an insect caught and enveloped in the web. The female spider then being occupied with the consumption of the gift, the male presses on with the sexual act and after that tries – not always successfully – to

A.L. Clément.

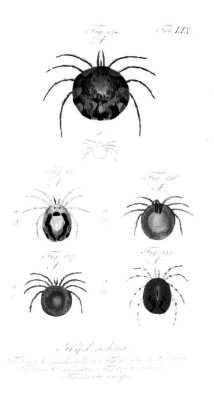

'Water mites' of the family *Hydrachna*, from Hahn's *Die Arachniden*.

escape. Sometimes the male even succeeds in snatching back his 'gift' in order to go with it to another female spider. There are however situations in which the female spider accepts the gift, but does not allow the male spider to proceed with the sexual act. Sometimes the intercourse ends in an act of erotic cannibalism in which the weaker male is subsequently chewed up. Though this happens only in some mating rituals, the universally known mythology of the Black Widow spider – which is based on real observations – refers to these murderous practices.

A twentieth-century engraving of a pair of silk-spiders of the genus *Nephila* (male top, female below).

However, research in autumn 2009 has shown that males who signal their erotic intentions by twanging the web harmoniously and for a long time have a greater chance of survival than other suitors – even when mating with aggressive man-eating females. It is a lesson which might incidentally also be applied to human erotic behaviour.

Despite its obvious predatory traits the female spider is on the whole a very caring mother. The laid eggs are ensconced carefully in a cocoon, creating a kind of egg sac, then camouflaged and deposited on the soil or hung up among foliage. This is the practice among orb weavers: other species go much further in their efforts. Some spiders carry the eggs with them on the body. The young are protected by their mothers and nourished by insects caught in the mother's web. Sometimes the insects are

Role-reversal: an *Aphonopelma* tarantula under threat from a 'tarantula hawk' wasp parasitical on tarantulas.

first chewed thoroughly by the mother, who subsequently puts the paste food into the mouths of the young. The mother–child relationship is however one-sided: there are cases – to mention here only an Australian spider species – when the young, after growing up, indulge in an act of matriophagy by paralysing their mother with poison and then consuming her when she is already much weakened. More often, however, the mother has already died and her children simply eat up her corpse. Only a few cases of caring fatherhood are known to arachnologists –

The Goliath bird-eating spider of South America.

one of these is provided by the *Bagheera kiplingi* found recently in
in the forests of Central America. The males help the mothers
look after their eggs and the young.

The majority of spiders prey on insects. Some giant spiders
enrich their diet with frogs, lizards and mices or even small birds.
They know very well how to prepare their repast: a captured frog
is swiftly reduced to a shapeless pulp. The aforementioned
Bagheera kiplingi seems to be the only truly vegetarian spider of
the world, being almost exclusively herbivorous.[5] However
from time to time even this exceptionally 'decent' spider has to
nibble on ant larvae in order to escape culinary monotony.
Recent research has shown that some spiders prefer to eat mosquitoes which are full of sucked blood, in contrast to mosquitoes
in their pure state.

The process by which the spider catches a victim possesses
a visual drama of its own and has since time immemorial provoked feelings of revulsion that have led to the spider's use in a
number of allegories in literature as well as politics. The most
popular proof of the spider's ensnaring and trapping faculties is
provided by the gummy orb web. The orb web has in its function
as a catching instrument an optimal relation between its width
– the wider it is, the greater the chances of catching an insect
therein – and the necessary holding strength of its threads, the
latter requirement preventing an overextension of the surface
of the web that might lead to breakage.

Responding to stimuli coming from the vibrations it registers
in the web, the spider is endowed with an innate ability to distinguish between potential victims and eventual threats. If he
comes to the conclusion that his attack has no chance of success
or might even endanger him the spider quickly cuts his own web
and retires instantly from the field of battle. The hunter sits in
the middle of the web or sometimes in a sort of corner, holding

The cover of an edition of J.-H. Fabre's *La Vie des Araignées*.

the thread, which signals and transmits even the slightest vibrations. The web also serves as a signalling relay. Some spiders use different sorts of vibrations to signal to their nearby offspring; by means of a pleasing, low-intensity vibration a spider can communicate that the prey has finally been killed and can now be safely consumed. On the other hand a short intense twanging usually conveys an message of imminent danger.[6]

The web is produced by short spinnerets with many spigots connected to one silk gland. The silk thus obtained is initially in liquid form, containing mostly proteins. It subsequently hardens both through exposure to air and by being drawn out longer and longer. Needless to say the silk produced by the spider differs greatly from that produced by the silkworm in its consistency and qualities.

The elastic qualities of the web are second to none – modern scientists are still astounded by its effortless combination of seemingly contradictory characteristics. The threads of the web are as elastic as nylon and show a tensile strength almost as great as that of steel, providing an unsurpassed model for the ever-ongoing search for new fibres and ropes. It was only in 2007 that a complicated X-ray screeening of the threads showed that they owe their elasticity and durability to the presence of so-called cristallites, which make up 20 per cent of the thread. When under pressure from stretching these cristallites align themselves longitudinally and gradually become creased, which means that more exterior energy is required to break them.[7] Thus paradoxically up to a certain (breaking) point the durability of the thread is strengthened. No doubt that present-day scientists would very much like to follow the example of inhabitants of the South Pacific islands, who use threads of the golden silk orb weaver (*Nephila clavipes*) to make their sturdy fishing nets.

Medical technology is nowadays experimenting with the use of special spider threads as an ultrathin stitching material to be used in neurosurgical operations. There are also plans to master the technique of using spider threads to repair links between ruptured or cut human nerve fibres.[8] Thus the analogy from antiquity that makes the link between the threads of the web and the nerves of the human body is borne out in modern science. (see chapter Three).

The universally known orb-web, as woven by *Araneus* spiders, is the product of a complicated building process. As a first step the

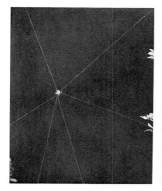

spider links two fixed points through a delicate thread hovering in the air. Then he starts to construct a sort of frame with a central point from which the radial and spiral construction are successively carried out. Upon reaching the frame the spider reverts in the direction of the centre but now with a closer spacing. The hub in the middle is much thicker and stronger than the rest of the web, serving both as an constructional nexus but also as the spider's lair, that is, as the particular location from which he controls the situation. A variant of the orb web posesses a strengthened hub and a stabilimentum: usually this is a thickened single line, but sometimes it takes the form of a St Andrew's cross. Despite the archetypal popularity of the orb-web we have to keep in mind the fact that only one-seventh of all webs are of the classic roundish type. Among the remaining webs we should mention the triangular webs made by *Hypiotes*, many funnel-shaped types, some baldachin forms, and webs that are like sheets. A number of webs have no great strength or adhesive power of their own, but rely on trip lines to catch and glue the unhappy insect.

Nearly every kind of orb web is woven in a different way, often making it possible to identify the spider species that wove

An early stage in spinning an orb-web.

Later it is clear how the orb-web hangs from a single thread.

The spider's web.

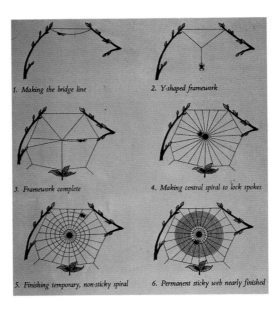

1. *Making the bridge line*

2. *Y-shaped framework*

3. *Framework complete*

4. *Making central spiral to lock spokes*

5. *Finishing temporary, non-sticky spiral*

6. *Permanent sticky web nearly finished*

it. Some species make their spirals zigzag, others leave the cones completely free. There are variations in the number of radii and in the distance between the spirals and great differences in the ornamentation. The ability to make the web being an inborn faculty, baby spiders produce as perfect a design as their parents. In normal circumstances spiders do not get stuck in their own nets, navigating the dry threads with great acumen and avoiding the adhesive force of the glue. A number of spiders are able to roll up their webs into a compact ball in a matter of seconds. Then they consume the silk, getting nourishment from micro-organisms trapped in it and obtaining by a sort of recycling the material needed for construction of a new web.

The overwhelming majority of spiders lead an isolated existence as solitary predators. There exists however a distinct subcategory of the Aranae, aptly named social spiders, which comprises some two dozen species. These live in sheet-web colonies and show an advanced level of cooperation. The great Stegodyphus family of social spiders appears both in South Africa and in the Mediterranean. There the mother feeds her offspring from mouth to mouth and is even ready to care for alien children. Earlier theories that social spider colonies are negatively influenced by permanent inbreeding have been disproved by recent research.

An impressive social spider colony in the Texan Lake Tawakoni State Park discovered in 2007 had a length of almost 200

'White-tailed Spider in his Web', from R. A. Ellis's 1913 book *Im Spinnenland.*

metres, blanketing quite a number of smaller trees and bushes. Cooperation takes place either in the classic mother–offspring form or as an extended cooperation between adult spiders. From a sociological point of view these spider colonies offer a fascinating glimpse into the problems of larger groupings both of animals and also – to an extent – of human habitations. On the one hand greater cooperation and breadth of the web allows the catching of more prey; on the other any reduction in the supply of food leads to internecine conflicts, often ending in cannibalistic acts. What is more, the high visibility of the colonies sometimes provokes aggression by large predators. The interior organization of the sheet web, with the stronger spiders residing near the safer centre and the smaller and weaker ones on the fringes, constitutes an arrangement which shows marked similarities with human situations.

Now we have to take up the most dramatic and spectacular aspect of the spider's existence, namely his mode of preying upon unsuspecting victims, the gummy orb-web being only one of several deadly instruments serving that purpose. Many spider types carry with them a kind of small net which they throw – when possible – on the victim. Other species 'spit' with parts of the web, thus gluing the victim firmly to the ground or to some other object such as a tree. However, since the spider is often much smaller and delicately built than his chosen victims, the web alone does not always suffice. In order to neutralize his prey

'Orb-weaver' spider-webs at Lake Tawakoni, Texas, in the summer of 2007.

swiftly most spiders use the neurotoxic poison manufactured in their glands. The poison is very fast-acting and can paralyse a victim that would seem to have the upper hand – such as the bumble-bee, which can be almost twenty times larger than its adversary – in a matter of seconds. Spiders use different preying techniques, the most popular being the 'swift bite and wrap'. Often, however, the so-called 'long bite', with the spider persevering with his sting, is used.

Small tunnels or caverns also provide a good place for ambushing insects – they can be swiftly drawn into the cavern and then paralysed. Some species attack by jumping on the victim from a distance of a dozen or so metres. These spiders often use an elastic thread-like rope functioning in a similar way to a modern bungee-rope. This technique allows the spider a speedy and secure return to his hideout after the attack, together with his paralysed prey.

Death does not come quickly to the spider's victims. The spider's fangs or *chelicerae* infuse a paralyzing poison into the captured insect, and the enveloping cocoon helps to hold the victim tightly and does not allow the weakened insect to flee. Thus the enveloping web or cocoon becomes a kind of larder, and the spider has for some time a readily available food at hand. In other cases where the victim is eaten up at once, the spider sprinkles the corpse with gastric juices, thus transforming it into an easily edible paste which the spider sucks into his small mouth opening. There are also species of underwater spiders who prey on small insects or on their larvae.

Much of the fear generated by spiders is based on the popular image of that animal as a poisoner. Though all spiders (with the sole exception of the Uloboridae) possess poison glands and use them in their attacks against larger insects, only some two dozen species out of the 40,000-odd known spider types

Banded Argiope (banded garden spider), *Argiope trifasciata*, with swathed prey, dorsal view.

constitute a real threat to humans. Thus only some exotic variants of the Black Widow, the Australian *Atrax Robustus*, the North American *Loxosceles reclusa* or the South American *Phoneurtia fera* – the last of which is found mainly on banana trees – can sting in a dangerous or even deadly manner. In Europe stings by a handful of local species might cause painful sensations of an intensity similar to the sting of a wasp or a bee, but no more than that.

The feelings of fear or revulsion generated by the spider are therefore induced by his looks, by his particular swift and silent mode of moving and catching the prey and also by his real – or reputed – cannibalistic sexual practices. These fears of course had a great deal of influence on the growth and spread of modern arachnophobia. But they are also to be found behind a great number of myths, images and psychological beliefs which cannot all simply be reduced to arachnophobia but which have their roots in a wider cultural, religious or psychological background. These fascinating phenomena we would like to discuss in the next chapters.

A nineteenth-century engraving of a Goliath bird-eating spider dining.

2 Arachnophobia

Most discussions or reflections in English on the grievous affliction of arachnophobia start with the well-known verse in Mother Goose.

> Little Miss Muffet
> Sat on her tuffet
> Eating her curds and whey
> There came a big spider
> And sat down beside her
> And frightened Miss Muffet away.

Regardless whether this little nursery rhyme was really written down in the early seventeenth century or, as some scholars claim, much later, in the years around 1800, it describes the fright of a young lady whose father, the Elizabethan clergyman Thomas Muffet, indulged in an excessive fondness for his house spider, which to his mind had 'beautifie[d] with her tapestry and hangings' the family house. Little Miss Muffet, as her reaction shows, held the opposite opinion.

It is generally thought that arachnophobia is an example of a biologically generated fear, whose roots go back to the anxieties of our pre-technological ancestors, with their vastly greater array of enemies and phobias and their associations of the

Little
Miss Muffet..

... sat on a tuffet
reading a picture book
there came a spider–
and sat down beside her
and said, "May I have a look"?

MADE BY ILLINOIS WPA ART PROJECT-CHICAGO

'Little Miss Muffet'
and her spider on
a 1940s American
poster.

spider with darkness and danger.[1] According to a number of
studies the spider invariably makes it to the top four or five on
the list of the most feared animals; it still loses out to the snake,
but the latter's virtual extinction in many civilized countries will
one day effect a change in that particular competition. Arachnophobia – as subtly implied by the Muffet rhyme – mostly affects

French erotic
imagery involving
a spider, from
c. 1900.

females, though the statistical ratio of nine afflicted women to
one arachnophobic man claimed by some writers seems to be
somewhat exaggerated.[2] The phobia obviously does not have
much to do with actual danger, since it is very much present in
countries with fairly innocuous spiders like Britain, a land where
one-third of women and almost 20 per cent of men express a
fear of spiders. Typical reactions to a spider by an arachnophobe
include screaming, trembling with fear, attacks of blind panic,
heart throbbing and – last but not least – nausea. Dramatic reactions include hitting out at random, running away in panic and
lapses into unconsciousness. To the domain of semi-rational
actions belongs the widespread practice of asking non-arachno-
phobes to remove the threatening spider from one's premises.

Nude woman in
a spider's web.

46

The fact that there is no consensus among arachnophobes as to the most frightening feature of the spider indicates that the primary reason for their fear is deeply hidden, and might have a polymorphous character.

On the other hand some mild arachnophobes show an obvious fascination with the spider, are able to look at images of it and might even be able to deal with the *frisson* of fear in the same way as they do with a good horror or mystery movie. But most arachnophobes dislike both living spiders and images of them: thus in 1913 the wife of Germany's then leading press magnate August Scherl expressly forbade her husband ever to print in his many journals a photo or a drawing of a spider. It seems that Lady Scherl's injunction was respected for quite a long time.

It is obvious that arachnophobia has few rational causes. Recent investigations have shown that people in Europe show less fear of being stung by a bee or wasp (whose stings produce almost a hundred deaths by allergic shock in Europe each year) than of being stung by a spider – the latter being a very rare occurrence and not at all threatening. It might be thus considered that arachnophobia is foremost an irrational attitude, referring to dangers unknown, since most people have been stung one time or another by a bee or wasp, whereas almost nobody has experienced the sting of a spider. Since potential harmfulness cannot thus account for arachnophobia, an explanation has to be sought foremost in the domains of symbolism and neurotic behaviour. Let us also mention the interesting fact that continents with very dangerous spiders like Australia or Southern America have few spider myths or tales.

Phenomenons like the famous 'tarantism' in the Italian province of Apulia were exercises in a semi-controlled mass hysteria directly referring to the bite of the 'venomous' tarantula spider. Becoming more prominent in the sixteenth century, the tarantula dance (known also as tarantella) lapsed into obscurity around 1900, though it has recently been revived as a folkloristic and touristic ploy. It symbolically reenacts both the spider's bite and a following cure through frenzied, dance-like moves. The dancing Apulians play out a ritual suggestive of a state of being gripped by dizziness and nausea. The tarantic rituals and dances in Southern Italy and some places further off have fascinated many ethnographers and cultural historians, since the tarantists – mostly women – also evoked by their movements a symbolic image of a biting spider. However, medical historians tend on the whole to disclaim any real causal line between a spider's supposedly venomous bite (the tarantula has no venom) and the reportedly 'stricken or bitten' population, seeing in the ritual the effect of suggestion, and the expression of a fear of real epidemics like the plague.[3]

In the developed world it is often the bathroom, with its white tiles amplifying the contrast with the black, crouching spider, that concretely localizes and embodies a hitherto rather vague

A tarantula from J.-H.Fabre's *Souvenirs Entomologiques* (1879–1907).

feeling of apprehension and transforms it into a violent outburst of fear. Thus the spider certainly functions as a kind of dark symbol, perceived in an almost Gestaltist way, since on seeing the stark black and white contrast many think of it as a sign presaging a dark menace to come. For people more heavily afflicted by arachnophobia the sight of a spider is a nightmare come true. Arachnophobia is often acquired in childhood and tends then to stay throughout one's whole life. It is also transmitted in families, especially when one of the parents cannot dissimulate his or her arachnophobic sentiments.

One of the reasons for the fear induced by the spider might be the fact that the spider is connected with that aspect of the widespread dislike of insects associated habitually with filth and uncleanliness. However it seems doubtful whether the spider really – as some proponents of the 'unclean theory' have suggested – was associated in medieval Europe with outbreaks of the bubonic plague. Though the spider is not an insect and shuns pedestrian locales in favour of the higher reaches he is nonetheless linked with untidiness by virtue of the fact that cobwebs indicate lack of window and wall cleaning, or indeed the lack of any cleaning effort whatsoever. Modernizers often talk of sweeping away cobwebs, but this metaphor is only indirectly connected with arachnophobia as such.

The spider displays a whole set of physical and behavioural characteristics which might provoke arachnophobic sentiments or acts. We mean here a general 'spideriness' as such, with words and descriptions like *hairy* or *creepy* tending to send shivers down the spine. But it is significant that most arachnophobes know quite a deal about the various habits of the spider and are openly or subconsciously afraid of stinging, bloodsucking, cannibalistic eroticism or being caught in a spider's net. Thus a good factual knowledge of the spider tends to stimulate even further bouts of irrationality. An important factor is an obsessive fear that somewhere in the room a spider is looking on the arachnophobe and watching his every step. What is more, even a preoccupation with spider symbolism does not immunize against arachnophobia. When writing the last pages of this book we learned that even the hero of recent *Spider-Man* films, the actor Tobey Maguire, suffers from arachnophobia and is therefore keen to undergo psychological counselling.

Many people explain their personal problems in terms of being caught or enmeshed by a mysterious net, a net closely resembling that of the spider, but with no visible main enemy. Thus the net assumes metaphysical qualities, embodying a cruel fate meted out by powers unknown. These fears are very vivid and poignant and they point to a paramount fear of the spider's manifold aggressive acts, regardless of whether the creature itself is visible or invisible. After passing that level of explanation we enter the domain of psychoanalytical explorations and references.

Here the most important explanative theory pertains to the *Urangst* (or primeval fear) men feel in relation to the Great Mother. The great German natural philosopher Paracelsus claimed that spiders issue forth from the menstrual blood of females, an idea that constitutes a link of sorts with the aforementioned 'unclean hypothesis'. A combination of arachnophobia and genital-fearing misogyny might also be seen in the not infrequent comparison, both visual and metaphorical, of gnarled female pubic hair to a spider's lair, some masculine fantasies even placing our arachnoid in the vulva. However in the twentieth century the psychological bearings of the spider image became associated both with the complex of matriarchy and its powers and even more with that of the cunning, scheming woman: the femme fatale. We shall try to sketch the outlines of this problem in the following chapters. The fact that the great majority of arachnophobes are women does not have to be opposed to that attempt at a explanation. Male arachnophobia constitutes a fascinating, though not very extensive phenomenon linked foremost to the fear of a dominating mother. Some of its psychoanalytical aspects will be discussed in chapter Five.

As regards psychological interventions and attempts to cure arachnophobia we can distinguish more or less between two approaches, the first one being a kind of shock therapy and the second aiming at a longer process of desensitivization. In the first approach the victims of arachnophobia are forced to kiss – through a glass panel – dead spiders placed in cases. This healing technique aims to accustom the suffering person to the sight of the eight-legged menacing creature. It is a kind of aversion therapy based mainly on exposure, but combined with expert psychological aid. The second approach aims at a desensitivization and was based initially on a confrontation by means of photographic spider images. The majority of the adherents of this approach have now renounced images as such, and the long training sessions attempt to conjure spider incursions onto one's body solely by force of the imagination. The fear and the feelings provoked by such imaginary attacks are then discussed in therapeutic sessions which reconstruct the sensations engendered by them through a step by step analysis.

Arachnophobia is thus foremost a malady of a febrile imagination. Shakespeare, who did not like spiders, knew this well. In *The Winter's Tale* (Act ii, scene i) he suggested that the fear caused by the spider arises in the imagination of the person afflicted and not from an actual experience of the spider or its venom:

There may be in the cup
A spider steep'd, and one may drink, depart,

and yet partake no venom, for his knowledge
is not infected; but if one present
the abhorr'd ingredient to his eye, make known,
How he hath drunk, he cracks his gorge, his sides,
With violent hefts.

3 Venom and Cold Intellect: The Spider and its Web in the European Intellectual Tradition

If there is one certain fact concerning the position of the spider in the long line of European thought, it is the relative predominance of interest in the web. That seemingly artificial product of the spider – or, viewed from another angle, its integral part – fascinates its beholders to this very day, though the various strands of its critical fortune often seem to go into disconnected or even contradictory directions. No analytic survey of the spider and its web in their important roles as cultural phenomena and visual metaphors belonging to the mainstream European intellectual tradition has been attempted until now, a circumstance that may excuse the somewhat fragmentary character of the following remarks.

For the ancient Hebrews both the spider and his web possessed distinctly negative connotations. Hypocrites and their misplaced confidence are likened in the Book of Job (8) to frail spider webs. Another important symbolic strand – the reference to venom and venomousness as inherent traits of that insect – was provided by the passage in Isaiah 59, which characteristically stated in the same breath that a sinner is hatching serpent's eggs and spinning spider webs: the latter are to no avail, because 'they cannot provide clothing'. In a variation of the latter strand, the cobweb functioned as an symbol of that which is discarded, of lost glory. Thus the prophet Hosea could assure his followers that one day the pagan idols would lose their power and become mere cobwebs (Hos. 27). A further negative symbolic concept originating from the imagery of the Old Testament was the comparison of a withdrawn, self-centred lifestyle intent on accumulating wealth and guarding one's riches with the 'house of a spider' (Job 27). This striking metaphorical image was from that time on often applied to wealthy misanthropes living in the manner of a recluse in their castles, in the hope of thus guarding their riches, a vain hope, since a spider's house served also as a symbolic paragon of instability and fleetingness. Here it was the Quran, linked by many threads with Judeo-Christian imagery, which provided a symbolic continuity of sorts, by stating that the unbelievers are as 'the likeness of the spider who buildeth a house: but the very frailest of all houses surely is the house of the spider'. (Sura XXIX).

Jewish authors of the Middle Ages went so far as to declare the spider the creature most hated by man.[1] An early Jewish diaspora legend claimed that a spider, by carrying fire, had aided the Romans in their destruction of the temple in Jerusalem. But even in this particularly negative tradition there are singular

The hypocrite's hope shall perish: his hope shall be cut off, and his trust shall be a spider's web – according to Job, 8:13-14, in this early 13th-century illuminated French *Bible moralisée*.

שממת

מה היא אומרת

A spider 'praising the Lord' in an 18th-century German-Jewish manuscript.

exceptions: in a wonderful illustration in a German-Jewish eighteenth-century illuminated manuscript it is the spider in the centre of his web that praises the Lord through the invocation of Psalm 150 ('Praise him upon the loud cymbals . . .'). Obviously the imposing web serves as a testimonial to God's creative potency and sense of beauty. As we shall see later, this wonderful image echoed a new Enlightenment sentiment about the aesthetic ramifications of natural history.

The ancients had a mostly negative view of spiders, though when surveying the many sources it becomes obvious that they didn't know much about the various species – four centuries of written descriptions had already passed before Pliny the Elder first mentioned the fact that spiders are endowed with eight legs. Spiders were thought to be mostly venomous, dangerous to men but also prone to killing their own kind (Aristotle). Their appearance presaged catastrophes like bad weather or floods. Spiders that covered statues of rulers or ensigns of power with their webs were seen as foretelling approaching power struggles and revolutions.

The perpetual oscillation between an aesthetic admiration for the spider's web as a stupendously delicate structure and rejection of it as a symbol of old, useless things starts with the two contradictory relevant passages in Homer's *Odyssey* (8,280; 16,35) and continues as an often repeated antinomy up to the present day. The great Athenian lawmaker Solon (*c.* 638–558 BC) was credited with the authorship of a celebrated comparison of the judicial system to a spider's web: the system and the courts can catch only insignificant transgressors as small insects or flies, greater insects and socially superior culprits can mostly force their way through the web of justice. The comparison was taken up by many authors, from antiquity to modern times, to name only the famous Proverbs of Erasmus. An excellent version can be found in an emblem epigram written by the seventeenth-century English poet George Wither:

> The nimble Spider from his Entrailes drawes
> a little Thread, and curious art doth show
> in weaving Nets, not much unlike those Lawes
> which catch Small-Thieves and let the Great-ones goe.[2]

The fact that more than 2,500 years after its first use this analogy is still being used to describe many judicial systems throughout the world cannot be a source of satisfaction to us.

Another popular cliché pertaining to the web was formulated by the Stoic philosopher Ariston, who compared the flowery orations of the dialectical school of rhetorics to a spider's web and

Von der Spinen vndgefatz.

Das ftarcker webfen keinen nöt/
Vnd kleiner mücklein vil ertödt.

declared them both to be artful, but in a deeper sense useless. Since that time the spider's web came to be associated with sophistry and dialectic, as in Paolo Veronese's splendid ceiling painting in the Sala del Collegio of the Doge's Palace (1578) in Venice.

The spider and his works served also as prime examples in the attempts of Stoic philosophers in the Hellenistic era to prove their theory that the sagacity of animals is due not to reason but to natural instinct. Already Aristotle had in his famous exposition of the teleological moment in nature (*Physics*, II, 8) referred to swallow nests and the web of the spider as good examples of the predominance of instinct over mind. An even better example of that tendency in natural philosophy provided the famous philosopher Philo of Alexandria with a lengthy account of the spider's way of life three centuries later.[3] Philo gave an enthusiastic description of the matchless art with which the web is made, pointing out that the spider knows no division of labour

and that it forms all parts alike without any assistance. Then he proposed an interesting analogy: as regards pride in his work and the anger he directs towards his enemies, among men only the artist is the spider's equal.

Philo's characterization of the spider as an artist might have been influenced by the written formulation of the legend – which in itself certainly went back to earlier, Hellenistic sources – of the Lydian weaver Arachne, a work undertaken by the great Roman poet Ovid in his famous *Metamorphoses* (VI, 5–145). Philo must have written his treatise sometime between AD 20 and 45, Ovid's *Metamorphoses* were composed between AD 2 and 8; the chronological coincidence, as regards the invention of the motif of the artist-spider, certainly would merit a more thorough analysis.

In a famous long passage of the poem Ovid described the superior weaving skills of Arachne, daughter of the wool-dyer Idmon, who lived in the Lydian town Hypaepa. Since the fifth century BC the documented Greek word for the spider was *arachne*; the legend was thus to provide *inter alia* an etymological rationalization.

Arachne's skills were so astounding that many visitors flocked to her workshop, many of them convinced that Arachne could not have attained all this without the help of Pallas Athena. Upon hearing these opinions, Arachne publicly stated that she had achieved everything on her own. To prove that and bolster her position she had the temerity to challenge the goddess to a weaving competition. Pallas Athena, appearing in the guise of an old woman, warned her and demanded an apology, which Arachne – blinded by pride and ambition – steadfastly refused. Furious, Pallas Athena assumed her real shape and accepted the foolhardy challenge. In the ensuing scene the literal sense of spinning and weaving overlaps with the metaphorical

concept of weaving associated with poetic composition in a masterly fashion.

In the tapestry which she wove with great speed, Pallas Athena showed the twelve Olympian Gods assembled around Jupiter, in the act of supporting her in a quarrel with Neptune. By depicting also on the tapestry a number of personages who in the past had outrageously challenged the Olympians and who were, in result, very severely punished by the gods, Pallas Athena had issued a direct last warning. Undeterred, Arachne wove with imposing speed a series of scenes showing the erotic adventures of Jupiter. From an artistic point of view Arachne's tapestries were masterly, but neither the choice of themes nor the fact that a mortal tried to demonstrate her creative superiority could go unpunished.

Angered by Arachne's haughty demeanour, Pallas Athena tore up the tapestries and struck her in the face three or four times

Johann Wilhelm Baur, *Pallas Athene changes Arachne into a Spider*, 1641, etching.

with the weaving spindle. Terrified by this outburst of anger, Arachne tried to hang herself, but the Goddess had decided otherwise: sprinkling Arachne with the poisonous juice from Hecate's herb, she had the Lydian girl transmogrified into a spider, destined from now on to hang on her own threads from the walls but also to continue her former craft of weaving in more modest surroundings. Athena expressly condemned Arachne and all the future generations of spiders to an unhappy existence.

If we undertake a structural analysis of the Ovidian Arachne-fragment we soon find there at its core four themes that were to shape the next two millennia of human views of the spider and his myth. There is the designation of the spider as an ugly and spiteful insect; the equivalence of the spider with the female; the connection of the spider with designs against the existing order; the lauding of her unparalleled abilities as an artistic weaver of webs and tapestries. Of course the importance of each strand varied in the course of history and each one was in time duly enriched by supplementary meanings.

However beside these major strands a number of supplementary points should be mentioned here. First of all Ovid raises here in a novel fashion, unknown to his contemporaries, the question of man's artistic strivings and the subsequent status of an artist, suggesting in the process that the tearing-up of the tapestry was tantamount with the death of Arachne, since the wretched Lydian girl had defined her existence solely in artistic terms. The fact that Ovid expressly refers to the blonde hairs of Pallas Athena in the moment when she is about to transmogrify Arachne into an obviously black spider is designed to deepen by means of an antonymic symbolic linkage the contrast between two figures who only a short time ago were introduced on seemingly equal terms. By referring to a belief of the popular pre-Ovidian Greek mythology according to which the 'noxious spiders have been born out of the blood of the Titans'[4] we can discover another, hitherto seemingly overlooked, brilliant symbolic ploy of the great Roman poet, since the goddess Hecate, whose herbal juice provided the poison for Pallas Athena that was needed to transform Arachne into a spider, had herself in earlier times been a Titan.

In the same book of the *Metamorphoses* Ovid describes – though in a much shorter fragment – the fate of the hapless Marsyas, who foolishly challenged Apollo to an artistic contest and was cruelly punished by the Sun God. Both Arachne and Marsyas were thus to symbolize both the human striving for artistic perfection and the problems arising from too great an ambition.

Ovid says expressly that Arachne as a spider continued her old weaving skills and thus he bestows on the spider's web a measure – but only a measure – of artistic perfection. The problem of the artistic or semi-artistic character of the spider's creation continued to crop up in later epochs. The late-antique writer Claudian described a half-finished, abandoned tapestry where only the spider was sacrilegiously weaving his own web, though the latter's web had no artistic value.[5] The great moralist Seneca argued differently, pointing out that the spider can weave a web so subtle that no man's hand could imitate it. But then Seneca draws a semi-philosophical distinction between nature and the work of art, thus continuing in a certain sense Aristotle's thesis of the predominance of instinct over mind: 'This art is born and not acquired by teaching . . . You will note that all spiders webs are equally fine . . . The products of art are . . . uneven, but nature's assignments are always uniform.'[6]

Ovid's lengthy narrative, which gave a literary foundation to the habitual admiration of the spider web's shape, later became one of the most known passages in the *Metamorphoses*. Antique

sources mention images depicting Arachne (none of which seem to have survived), and the story of Arachne was taken up in illustrations in the late Middle Ages and depicted often in the modern era, to mention here only Velázquez' famous *Hilanderas* (*c.* 1657, now in the Prado, Madrid). The scene in the foreground shows spinning and weaving women, the scene before the tapestry in the background – as the great iconologist Aby Warburg and later independently Enriqueta Harris were first to discover – depicts both Pallas Athena and Arachne gesticulating vividly. It is conceivable that the great Spanish painter intended here an artistic allegory based on the major lines of Ovid's artistic ideology.[7]

Another interesting tradition was the one originating with the famous pre-Socratic philosopher Heraclitus of Ephesus which tried to compare the sensory faculties of man and the spider. In discussing the relation of the soul and the body, Heraclitus remarked that

> like a spider sitting in the middle of his web and reacting swiftly, as if personally aggrieved by the loss of some threads, to any destruction of his web caused by a fly, so the human soul wanders swiftly after the injury sustained by a part of her body to that part, as if she would be aggrieved by the mutilation of her body with whom she is linked in a particular relationship.[8]

Heraclitus' formulation was taken up almost three centuries later by the Stoic philosopher Chrysippus (c. 280–c. 206 BC), who, influenced by the recent discovery of the nervous system, created a model of the body with a central organ located in the heart (*Hegemonikon*) and seven parts of the body linked with it by impulses travelling through tensile parts. Chrysippus reframed the idea of Heraclitus and stated that 'as the spider sitting in the centre of the web feels the moment when a fly comes into it, so the *hegemonikon* sits in the heart and feels the impulses transmitted by the senses'.[9] This was a very important empirico-philosophical concept and, going further, an image which was to provide the basis of all the analogies of the web to the nervous and sensory faculties of the human body. As such it has found an imposing revival in some of the metaphors surrounding today's World Wide Web. Moreover this Greek concept was now applied to an Old Testament passage – an emblematic act, and one that seems interestingly enough to have utterly escaped the attention of biblical philologists – namely to the Greek translation of the Old Testament, the Septuagint. Into Psalm 38 the translator introduced – only some decades after Chrysippus's analogy of the body's sensory structure with the web – a comparison of the 'drying up of a sinner's soul' with the supposed dryness of the spider's web. The original Hebrew text, speaking about the way a moth attacks clothing as a metaphor of life fleeing from the body, doesn't mention a spider at all. These images of decay and death also referred implicitly to Chrysippus' overall concept, creating a fascinating link between Jewish and Greek Stoic thought. The comparison of a dying man's body to the limbs of a spider was to become a commonplace image in the naturalistic and symbolist literature of the nineteenth century.

Despite these supplementary associations the Old Testament tradition portrayed the spider's web as a weak, transitory structure and thus created a motif recurrent in early Christian thought.

For Ambrose (*Enarrationes in Psalmos*)[10] the spider is a prime example of a mindless industriousness, since he works on his web day and night without achieving anything usable in the form of clothing. Going further, Ambrose compares the spider with diligent men who, by devoting themselves totally to work and the pursuit of riches, neglect the exigencies of Christian spiritual life. Ambrose combined and developed here two biblical motifs, one from Isaiah (59) and one from the Vulgate's laconic translation of Psalm 89, where the years pass by 'in vain, spider-like labours'. Together with the melancholy motif of the weblike frailty of human life, these negative images and references were to dominate Christian attitudes in the first millennium and later. Thus in the late Middle Ages we can find an interesting variation of the image invoked in the Septuagint rendering of Psalm 38, when some theologians compared the evanescence of the soul with the evanescence of the spider due to his spinning out the web from his 'own entrails'.[11]

The first Christians took up the web's intrinsic paradox in its Solonic variant, namely that it can catch small flies, but that it can't pose an obstacle to larger insects or creatures. Basil the Great, speaking up against pagan sophistry and philosophy, stated that despite their weblike artful nature – this an obvious echo of Ariston's celebrated comparison – they could catch and ensnare only small 'flies'. More important at that time however was the comparison of the enemies of true Christianity, namely the first opponents of the established church – labelled now as heretics – to spiders. This was an image engendered no doubt by the still prevalent popular myth of the spider's venomous capabilities and by the web's potential to ensnare and to entangle, providing a powerful symbolic image of a permanent threat to weak Christian souls.

Basil's comparison of the heretics with a spider's web became the nucleus of the subsequent astounding career of the image, during which it became associated not only with religious dissent but also with political scheming and intrigues. Louis XI of France ('spider of Europe'), Philip II of Spain (the menacing 'spider of the Escorial', whose net strove without success to entangle good Queen Bess of England) and countless other political figures were faced with that accusation and characterized or caricatured accordingly. But nothing is simple in the domain of spider symbolism: leaving aside the problem of entrapment and subterfuge it was conversely, as proclaimed by a seventeenth-century emblem, the duty of a wise and diligent monarch to emulate the spider and stay, when exercising power, '*in centro*': in the centre of his web of governance. In this case the web is analogized in a positive way to a network that can transmit information and power.

But the negative symbolism weighed more heavily. In the last two centuries the spider's web has come to symbolize the murky world of right-wing political intrigues, as described in Joseph Roth's prophetic novel about the formation of Nazism, *The*

Spider's Web (1923), and of course it is an apt metaphor for the growing world of espionage. The web as a political image possessed a dual logic: though primarily destined to illustrate the entrapment of innocent people, it also depicted the business of gathering and transmitting information from the margins to the centre of the web. In its first function it had a potent metaphoric rival in the image of the octopus, with its far-reaching and versatile tentacles, though the octopus used naked, brute force in place of the spider's cunning and subterfuge.

Only one important early Christian thinker living in the sixth century, the redoubtable Cassiodorus, ventured a new arachnoid analogy by putting forward a novel, positively meant variant of the spider's significance.[12] According to him, like a spider who eschews the lowly earth and lives in the higher echelons of houses and trees, producing there from his own entrails subtle threads, so should the tired and fatigued Christian soul elevate itself by means of contemplation and turn its pure intellect towards God.

It is obvious that Cassiodorus makes here an analogy between intellectual operations and the spinning out of the spider's web, and the spider's tendency to lead a reclusive life in remote corners might have appealed to his anchoritic instincts – these are concepts which were to return many years later in a different context. But even theologians ready to acknowledge the delicacy of the web did not do it in unreserved terms. Thus Thomas Aquinas remarked in his commentaries on Aristotle's *Physics*[13] that man can – in contrast to the somewhat monotonous creativity of the spider – produce incessantly new forms, a perceptive remark that slightly modified Seneca's ideas and was later to find its way into Renaissance art theory.

The epoch of Aquinas witnessed also the rise of another important symbolic image. The popular conviction, deriving from antique sources, that the bite of the spider is particularly painful and – what was more important – that the spider is very quick to bite (here we can see an obvious influence of the aforementioned theories comparing the functioning of the human sensory and nervous systems to that of the spider) led in the thirteenth century to its choice as an attribute of the sense of touch (*tactus*) in images or image-cycles depicting the five senses.

A much quoted verse of the Dominican Thomas of Cantimpré formulated in his *Opus de naturis rerum* (1236–1250) a whole set of comparisons of the five senses with respective animals chosen for their sensory facilities. According to Cantimpré, as regards his five senses man is excelled by many creatures; eagles and lynxes have clearer vision, monkeys keener taste, vultures a more acute sense of smell, spiders a swifter touch, moles or the wild boar a more sensitive hearing. Hence the lines: *Nos aper auditu, linx visu, simia gustu, vultur odoratu praecellit, aranea tactu* (the boars excels us in hearing, the lynx in sight, the monkey in taste, the vulture in smell, the spider in touch). We find an interesting early example of the spider as a symbol of touch in the English allegorical mural painting in Longthorpe Tower, Peterborough (*The Five Senses,* around 1340).[14] This particular symbol gained a certain popularity in the sixteenth and at the beginning of the seventeenth century, foremost in German and Netherlandish engravings.[15]

Shakespeare evidently did not like spiders. In the *Midsummer Night's Dream* he wants the spiders to go away: 'Weaving Spiders, come not here; Hence, you long-legg'd spinners, hence'. He took up also the traditional association with venom and poisoning, speaking appropriately in *King Richard II* of spiders 'that suck up thy venom'. On the other hand he registered in a longer passage in the *Winter's Tale* – as mentioned already –

the excesses of arachnophobia and in this case puts the blame squarely on too fertile an imagination.[16] In Leonardo's *Animal Fables and Legends,* the spider plays a prominent, though pronouncedly negative role.[17] He is shown as an aggressive insect prone to transgressing the rules of social behaviour, forever paying for that a heavy price. The view of the spider as an withdrawn, aloof creature must have influenced Leonardo's vision of antisocial behaviour.

During the Counter-Reformation the spider provided a convenient symbol for a characterization of the interplay of the designs of the Devil with the actions of heretics; the unravelling of the spider's web was seen as a symbolic equivalent of the defeat of heresy. In a celebrated treatise published in Brussels in 1595 with the telling title *Kettersche spinnecoppen* (Heretical spiders), the leading Flemish Jesuit theologian Ioannes David compared both the Devil and the Protestants to spiders, with the difference however, that in David's imagery the Devil functioned as the primeval great spider, continually breeding lesser spiders in the form of heretics.

Thus it is not surprising that in a number of paintings showing the *Adoration of the Magi,* to refer here only to Rubens's splendid 1624 altarpiece from Antwerp (now in the Royal Museum), a prominent spider in the centre of a cobweb refers to the Devil and to heretics, both then and in the future to be overcome by Christ's birth and the ensuing era of grace and salvation.[18] In the Rubens painting the web is attached to a dark rough beam which contrasts with the glorious white column symbolically standing for the column of the Passion, consigning the spider to the role of a symbol for the outlived order of the Old Covenant.

Nothing, however, is simple in the domain of the symbolism of the spider. Though most religious thinkers, save Cassiodorus,

Wheel of the Five Senses mural painting with the spider symbolizing touch, Longthorpe Tower, Peterborough, *c.* 1340.

thought him reprehensible, there were also some things that could be said in his favour. In 1686 the famous Puritan writer John Bunyan published an educational emblem book, *A Book for Boys and Girls: or Country Rhymes for Children*, where different human characters or modes of life were set in analogy to various animals.[19] Somewhat unexpectedly we encounter here a dialogue between the allegorical 'Sinner' and the 'Spider', a dialogue characterized by the fact that the Sinner's first abhorrence at the sight of the 'venomed thing' gives way to a growing awareness that it is the Sinner himself who is the more repugnant of the two. The dialogue starts with a dramatic exchange:

> Sinner: What black? What ugly crawling thing thou art?
> Spider: I am a spider –
> Sinner: A Spider, Ay, also a filthy creature
> Spider: Not filthy as thyself, in name or feature.
> My name entailed is to my creation,
> My features from the God of thy salvation.

The Spider then admits – not without malice (one can discern here an influence of the Puritan anti-aesthetic prejudice) – that in so far as he is ugly and venomous he bears some resemblance to man; however there are, as he says, deeper symbolic resemblances. So the spider's web, symbolizing the empty pleasures he enjoys and the flimsy hopes of salvation he still cherishes, will point out to the Sinner the path to hell. But upon deeper reflection the Sinner should see and model his conduct on the persistence and determination with which the spider can find its way into the palaces of kings. This steadfastness and ambition should be a model for the Sinner in his search for Heaven. Bunyan's Puritan view of the child's duties did not impede the resounding impact of his book in the years up to 1800. A possible

Georg Pencz, 'Touch' from a series of *The Senses*, c. 1530, engraving.

TACTVS

SEDARANEATACTV

factor in the symbolic reappraisal of our insect was the spider's obvious industriousness, a trait dear to Puritan hearts.

Antique and medieval descriptions of the manifold spider families often included a comparison with other industrious insects, like the ant and the silkworm. The occasional comparisons with the silkworm stressed the benefits that men could derive from the positive industriousness of the silkworm, in contrast to the spider's web. A deeper significance and ideological relevance gained however only one such antonymic pair, namely the symbolic opposition between the spider and the bee. From the middle of the fourteenth century, when it appeared for the first time in Germany, till the middle of the eighteenth century, this comparison was destined to play – in its different

Johann Heinrich Campe, 'The Spider and the Silkworm', illustration for his *Kinder Abeze* (Braunschweig, 1806).

variations – a fascinating role in cultural life and literature. In Greek and Roman classical poetological thinking the industrious bee served as a common example of the most important mode of literary production: the collecting of 'literary ambrosia' with great discernment from different flowers and turning it into a new literary honey. The spider stood for a different principle, since according to popular belief he aggressively collected juice from sweet flowers – often harming them in the process – and then turned everything he had collected into venom. Thus the spider was posed as a paragon of venomousness and this very arbitrary tradition was continued right into the eighteenth century on the basis of a convenient symbolism.

The opposition of the spider and the bee was thus a striking example of the puzzle that 'if two do the same, the results do not have to be the same'. Many emblems of the sixteenth and seventeenth centuries that showed in the middle a rose flanked by a spider and a bee illustrated this rather simple, though still puzzling truth. The comparison lent itself to use by Catholic controversialists, since it could serve as a refutation of the Protestant claim that their confession had a base in the Bible. The Protestants as heretical spiders could gain no spiritual nourishment from their biblical lectures, since everything they collected from the Scriptures was transformed in their minds immediately into venom. On the other hand a thoughtful or religiously firm reader could profit even from reading a disputable book. The latter argument had no strictly confessional character, though it was used more by Protestants. The Elizabethan writer George Gascoigne declared in 1575:

And as the venemous spider will sucke poison out of the most holesome herbe, and the industrious Bee can gather hony out of the most stinking weede: Even so the discrete reader may take a happie example by the most lascivious histories, although the captious and harebrained heads can neither be encouraged by the good, nor forewarned by the bad.[20]

A more important aspect of the antonymic opposition of bee and spider concerned the comparison of the modes of action of both insects with the styles of creation in science and literature.

Israhel van Meckenem, 'The Spider and the Bee', c. 1490, detail from an ornamental engraving.

76

EMBLEMA LXXXII.
ARANEVS LACERTVLI
OS FILO OBLIGANS, PRIVS-
QVAM ILLVM MACTET.

Prius ora ligo, tum macto.

Auant que mon venin le touche
I'ay soing de luy fermer la bouche.

82.

A Nte lacertorum conſtringit Araneus ora,
    Quam morſu inſpiret virm , eoſque neces.

Albert Flamen,
emblem from
*Devises et
Emblesmes d'Amour*
(Paris, 1672).

We can find an excellent description of that problem on the pages of Francis Bacon's famous treatise *Novum Organum* (1624):

> Those who have handled sciences have been either men of experiment or men of dogmas. The men of experiment are like the ant: they only collect and use. The reasoners resemble spiders, who make cobwebs out of their own substance. But the bee takes a middle course; it gathers its material from the flowers of the gardens and of the field, but transform and digests it by a power of its own. Not unlike this is the business of philosophy . . .[21]

Paulus Aertsz. van Ravestein, The Spider as Reason, the Bee as Spirit in a woodcut from *Sleutel-bloem Vergadert . . . vit de Schriften van Jacob Boehme* (Amsterdam, 1635).

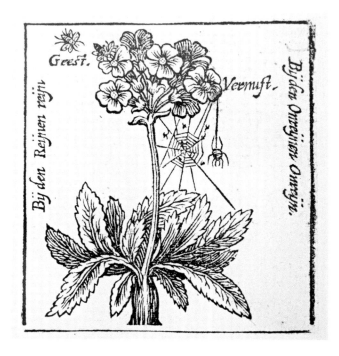

The reserved stance that Bacon – himself a famous empiricist – displayed towards the philosophical practice of 'spinning totally out of oneself' gave way in the seventeenth century to a philosophical speculation modelled on the *modus procedendi* of the spider, which also implied a break with the hitherto negative view of the creature, since it came to be seen as a kind of demiurgic constructor. Already in Bacon's time a love sonnet by Edmund Spenser posed the spider in a new role: the great poet likened himself to a spider conceived as a symbol of the overall principles of poetic composition, a spider that tries to catch the bee unaware (the bee symbolizing the beloved Elizabeth Boyle).

The woman to be caught in the spider's loving threads represents the literary procedure of collecting from different sources and amalgamating them into a new whole; the spider stands for the superior task of ordering the whole sonnet cycle. In the end they both happily come to an erotic agreement and 'thensforth eternall peace shall be, between the spyder and the gentle bee'. The fact that Spenser referred in his other writings twice to Arachne's tapestry (for example in *The Faerie Queene)* thus has to be seen in a wider literary context.[22]

In a formal sense the culmination of the motif was brought about by Jonathan Swift's *Battle of the Books* (1704), a magnificent depiction of a fictional battle in St James's Library in London between books representing ancient authors and those which were written by modern writers; the former group was represented by the bee, the latter the spider. Swift's sympathies were on the side of the ancients, as the following quotation vividly shows:

> For pray Gentlemen, was ever any thing so modern as the spider in his air . . . in his paradoxes ? He argues with many boastings and great genius, that he spins and spits wholly from himself and scorns to own any obligation or assistance from without . . . As for us we are content with the bee . . . with [her] infinite labour.[23]

Though Swift clearly opts here for the literary compilationary technique of the bee, the subsequent course of European literature was to rely more on the procedures of the spider. In his epoch Swift was seconded by the pre-Romantic poet Edward Young, who warned in his famous *Night Thoughts* (1745) against the danger that we

Spider-like, spin out our precious All,
Our more than vitals spin (if no regard
To great futurity) in curious Webs,
Of subtle Thought, and exquisite Design;
(Fine Net-Work of the Brain!)[24]

The analogy of the literary work to a cobweb mostly had a negative connotation, however, even in later times. Somerset Maugham once made the acerbic observation that Henry James's fictions are 'like the cobwebs which a spider may spin in the attic of some old house, intricate, delicate and even beautiful, but which at any moment the housemaid's broom with brutal common sense may sweep away.'[25] We find here in a concentrated form all the inherent clichés of that particular symbolic strand.

Whether all the anecdotes describing Spinoza's passion for spiders (he reportedly looked with a magnifying glass at spiders capturing flies and also seems to have organized spider fights) are to be taken at face value is difficult to say, though in an act of homage an interesting spider species has been named after the great seventeenth-century Dutch-Jewish philosopher. For Spinoza the demonstrable rationality of the spider's web was indicative of the principles of nature's geometry, an observation consonant with the philosopher's semi-pantheistic agenda and one with which he alluded, perhaps unconsciously, to the Asian motif of God as the great spider who orders the world. A century later the German philosopher Hamann said of systematic thinkers in the mould of Spinoza that they act like a group of 'rational spiders'. In the complicated allegoric anti-Enlightenment ceiling decoration painted in 1794 in the convent library at Strahov (Prague) by the great Baroque fresco painter Franz Anton Maulbertsch, an allegory of faith was placed compositionally above a negatively meant figure of an Enlightenment philosopher who is leaning on a telling attribute – a stone with a spider's web exposing a fly caught therein.[26] Maulbertsch's allegory thus connects the old anti-heretical early Christian and Counter-Reformational topoi with the web's role as a symbol of pure thinking.

In the eighteenth century attitudes toward the spider changed fundamentally. Though the myth of the spider's venomousness survived on the popular level well into the twentieth century, later being reinforced by information about dangerous tropical spiders, the first professional zoologists and enlightened public opinion – to refer only to the relevant article in the French *Encyclopédie* – now knew that European spiders were generally quite harmless.[27] The traditional, mostly theologically founded negative arachnoid symbolism gradually disappeared. A new theologico-philosophical tendency looking for the imprints of God in nature, continuing some strands of Spinoza's thought, discovered in the astounding structure of the spider's web the ordering hand of the Great Architect. One of the leading writers and philosophers of the French Enlightenment, Denis Diderot, used the image of the spider's web in his famous *Le Rêve de d'Alembert* as a model of the nervous and sensory system of humans and animals.[28] Diderot took up the Greek tradition initiated – as we tried to show earlier – by Heraclitus and Chrysippus and fused it with the fledgling sensualist philosophy of the Enlightenment.

Diderot attemped however in the *Rêve* to combine ideas about God as the Creator of the world proceeding 'like a spider' without any ruptures and without the influence of external factors. He ascribed the genesis of this image to Sufic Mohammedan philosophy – with a geometrical-creational thinking of the Spinozean type. As a result we are privy in the *Rêve* to a wonderful conversation between the sceptical physician Bordeu and Mademoiselle de l'Espinasse, during which Mademoiselle states boldly that one should take into account the possibility that

Franz Anton Maulbertsch, an Enlightenment philosopher with a stone and a spider's web, 1794, mural painting. Strahov convent, Prague.

somewhere in space 'resides a great or small spider, whose threads reach out everywhere'.[29] However the logic of this analogy implies also in the words of the all-knowing Bordeu, who functions here as a mouthpiece of Diderot, that God the spider and his web will have to share the material vicissitudes of our universe and accordingly die with it one far off day. The spider motif served Diderot for a courageous staging of biological materialism that went beyond the static metaphor of the web espoused by earlier philosophers and integrated the web model into a dynamic process of growth, decline and death.

Thus we can agree with the important French literary historian Georges Poulet that 'the symbol of the spider in its web greatly pleased the thinkers of the eighteenth century', since it showed that 'the perceptive faculties were being felt unitively . . . this unification of experience takes place at the center which is organized for it . . .'.[30] In a similar vein Montesquieu took up – in contrast to Diderot – the Greek tradition by stating that the soul in our body exists exactly like a spider in his net. She cannot move without vibrating one of the widely strung threads, in the same way as one cannot touch one of the threads without setting the spider in motion.[31]

Alexander Pope expressed an empiric version of that idea in an intellectually more mundane, but poetic way:

The spider's touch, how exquisitely fine!
Feels at each thread, and lives along the line.[32]

The Baroque had brought a resurgence of the aesthetic admiration for the spider's web. The Italian poet Tommaso Gaudiosi described around 1670 in his poem *La Ragna* (The Spider) the web as a work of art, with a sun-like centre and its threads brilliantly reflecting or carrying the rays.[33] However, with a characteristic baroque feeling for transience, Gaudiosi described a gust of wind destroying that glory in one single moment. The following century saw the web in a different light and tended to forget for a while its inherent fragility.

For the German pre-Enlightenment poet Barthold Brockes the mere sight of a spider's web constituted a supreme example of God's will to endow even the smallest and frailest parts of nature with beauty and a logical order.[34] The eighteenth-century Jewish Psalm illustration shown earlier had after all presented a similar message, as did a very interesting engraving from the *Physica sacra* (1731–5) by the Swiss early natural scientist Johann Jakob Scheuchzer. Here the giant spider's web in the foreground provides a sort of rational model for God in his work of creating the world. Orthodox Protestants attacked Scheuchzer vehemently for his attempts to present the Bible in the light of the ascending natural sciences.

This new openness towards the aesthetic side of the web can also be interpreted as a corollary of the rise of pantheistic sentiments. As regards the imagery of the spider in the strict sense, this sentiment was destined to bear its richest fruits with a somewhat surprising delay of more than two centuries. Only in the decades after 1970 did many religious posters or covers of religious pamphlets in Europe and America show stereotypal close-up photographs of a sun-lit or slightly dewy web in an overt reference to the role of God as a supreme designer of nature's wonders. The spider's web thus stands for the harmony of life, and the disquieting negative strand seemed over.

The vision of the spider in William Blake's writings stands apart from these general themes.[35] Blake drew in his illustrated poem *Europe* (1794) wonderful, if somewhat mysterious spider colonies; in his dream visions white and black spiders keep fighting for his soul. Often he describes spiders in a sympathetic way, using traditional attributes like industriousness. However, for Blake the spider becomes, when transporting meanings and exercising functions imparted on him by humans, a preposterous if not threatening creature, whose pretensions to organize vast spaces are doomed from the very beginning, so when Urizen (*The Four Zoas*) tries to bind 'all futurity . . . in his vast chain' he appears as if

Spiders, and other 'moving creatures that hath life', in C. A. Lesueur's illustration of Genesis I:20 in Johann Jakob Scheuchzer, *Physica Sacra* (1737).

Travelling thro darkness & wherever he traveld a dire web
Followed behind him as the Web of a Spider dusky & cold.

Thus the image of the web as an organizing, quasi-religious force is questioned in Night Eight of *The Four Zoas* when Urizen as the new spider fatally 'tangles in his own net'. Blake's thoughts and images here presage Romanticism in many ways, but are also related to older semi-mystic Swedenborgian strands.

TAB. XII.

GENESIS cap.I v.20.

I. Buch Mosis Cap.I.v.20.

Opus quintæ Diei.

Fünfftes Tagwerck.

J.A. Corvinus sculp.

Before we end, we should mention here one more special strand, which straddles successive epochs from the Renaissance to Romanticism and concerns the use of the motif of the spider web as an attribute of melancholy. The symbolic connection was provided here by the popular conviction that artists and intellectuals are children of Saturn – *inter alia* also known as the God of Melancholy – and that the spider's web stands for a particular melange of intellectual operation and innate artistry. Speaking about melancholy, which afflicted his old age, Michelangelo complained in one of his sonnets 'about breading a spider web in his ear'.[36] An anonymous drawing from the same time (1530–40, Paris, Ecole des Beaux-Arts) shows a spider's web hovering over a brooding melancholic, a motif taken up three centuries later in Caspar David Friedrich's famous 1804 woodcut *Melancholy*, where the web has a very forceful presence.

Baudelaire in his *Fleurs du mal* (1861) struck a similar note by using in the famous last poem (LXXVIII), a poem closing the *Spleen* cycle, the poignant negative metaphoric image of silent spider colonies and their webs in the poet's brain in order to describe a monotonous, ever deepening despair. We render here Baudelaire's beautiful verse in a somewhat pedestrian, but very literal translation:

When the long lines of rain
are like the bars of a vast prison
and a silent swarm of loathsome spiders
spin their nets at the bottom of my brain[37]

Baudelaire, who probably wrote this particular passage in 1857, may have been inspired by a somewhat similar spider metaphor in the *Contemplations* of Victor Hugo (1856),[38] but as an expression of mental depression this very image goes back –

Spiders from Thomas Martyn's 1793 *Aranei . . .*

And the clouds & fires pale roll'd round in the night of Enitharmon
Round Albions cliffs & Londons walls; still Enitharmon slept.
Rolling volumes of grey mist involve Churches, Palaces, Towers:
For Urizen unclasp'd his Book: feeding his soul with pity
The youth of England hid in gloom curse the pained heavens; compell'd
Into the deadly night to see the form of Albions Angel
Their parents brought them forth & aged ignorance preaches canting,
On a vast rock, perciev'd by those senses that are clos'd from thought:
Bleak, dark, abrupt, it stands & overshadows London city
They saw his bony feet on the rock, the flesh consum'd in flames:
They saw the Serpent temple lifted above, shadowing the Island white:
They heard the voice of Albions Angel howling in flames of Orc.
Seeking the trump of the last doom

Above the rest the howl was heard from Westminster louder & louder:
The Guardian of the secret codes forsook his ancient mansion
Driven out by the flames of Orc; his furr'd robes & false locks
Adhered and grew one with his flesh, and nerves & veins shot thro them
With dismal torment sick hanging upon the wind: he fled
Groveling along Great George Street thro' the Park gate; all the soldiers
Fled from his sight: he drag'd his torments to the wilderness.

Thus was the howl thro Europe!
For Orc rejoic'd to hear the howling shadows
But Palamabron shot his lightnings trenching down his wide back
And Rintrah hung with all his legions in the nether deep

Enitharmon laugh'd in her sleep to see (O womans triumph)
Every house a den, every man bound; the shadows are fill'd
With spectres, and the windows wove over with curses of iron:
Over the doors Thou shalt not; & over the chimneys Fear is written:
With bands of iron round their necks, fasten'd into the walls
The citizens: in leaden gyves the inhabitants of suburbs
Walk heavy: soft and bent are the bones of villagers

Between the clouds of Urizen the flames of Orc roll heavy
Around the limbs of Albions Guardian, his flesh consuming.
Howlings & hissings, shrieks & groans, & voices of despair
Arise around him in the cloudy
Heavens of Albion. Furious

a circumstance which seems to have been overlooked until now – to the aforementioned sonnet by Michelangelo, translated into French only in 1840 and probably known to the poet. Baudelaire might have also known the fact that, to quote here only the second edition of the *Encyclopedia Britannica* (1778, vol. I, p. 391), the membraneous *pia mater* surrounding the brain 'is usually described as being composed of two laminae, of which the exterior one is named *tunica arachnoides*, from its supposed resemblance to a spider's web'. However we should note here the fact that the French colloquial expression 'd'avoir une araignée au plafond' (to have a spider under the cranium, sometimes rendered in English under the pleasing rhyme of 'having a geranium under the cranium'), which suggests by means of an almost identical metaphor a kind of madness, had originated in the second part of the nineteenth century among Parisian prostitutes, a milieu Baudelaire knew very well.

Victor Hugo used yet another spider image in his *La Légende des siècles* (1857).[39] The great French late Romantic poet has the spider's web go without end into the vast expanses of heaven, this image being meant by him as a symbolic representation of endlessness, of melancholy and the metaphysical anguish in each of us. Going further, the poet compares the spider, alluding to its ray-like webs and circular structure, to the sun, though it is a sun shorn of its usual sparkling brilliance, a sun functioning in a certain sense even as a *soleil noir*: a black sun. Hugo might have been influenced here by the baroque tradition that claimed the spider as a symbol of the element of *air*.

As we can see, the amplitude of arachnoid symbolic references *chez Hugo* is an exceedingly wide one. His point of departure was marked by a quintessential romantic aesthetical contrariness, the poet declaring loudly to love the spider and the stinging nettle – needless to say this is a very interesting combination –

William Blake, from *Europe: A Prophecy*, 1794, hand-coloured etching.

because most other people happen to hate them. He sees the spider as a force of destiny. In a gripping scene in *Notre-Dame de Paris*, the Archdeacon impedes an attempt by Maître Jacques to liberate a captive fly from the web by exclaiming:

> Here you have a symbol of all that. [The fly] flies, she is happy, she awaits springtime, she looks for fresh air, for freedom. Oh yes, suddenly she encounters that fatal 'rose window', the spider crouches in it, a most ugly spider! The poor fly meets her preordained fate . . . Maître Jacques, do not intervene! This is fate . . . [40]

In that passage we note another visually stunning comparison of the web, namely to the rose windows of Gothic cathedrals. The reference to the rose windows strongly suggests, like the earlier declaration of love for stinging nettles, that Hugo saw the spider as a sort of 'Gothic' creature, both ugly and fascinating.

If considered in direct reference to the arachnoids as a species, the Hugoean spider represents also a kind of danger stemming from the insect's existence as a proverbially romantic *inconnu noir*. A drawing by Hugo which shows a skull with spiders might serve as a fascinating reassumption of motifs current both in Baudelaire's *Spleen LXXVIII* – after all, a skull too was evoked there by the poet in lines which directly preceded the 'spiders in the brain' metaphor. Other drawings by Hugo associate the spider with wanton destruction.

Interestingly enough, almost at the same time, in 1858, the famous historian Jules Michelet devoted to spiders two moving chapters of his entomological narrative *L'insecte*. Michelet's descriptions are on the whole very affective and tend to anthropomorphize the psychology of the spider. Whether Michelet was influenced by Hugo – the latter's vision is much more acerbic

Caspar David Friedrich, *Melancholy*, 1804, woodcut.

– is open to question, but the fact that France's foremost minds and poets showed in the 1850s a far-reaching fascination for arachnoids is in itself remarkable.

But these examples, though fascinating as regards their symbolic and artistic aspects, constituted by the middle of the nineteenth century only a sideline in the spider's cultural and intellectual history. To return to the main thread of that history, we should recapitulate the fact that the Enlightenment had 'de-demonized' the spider and conceived of him as an pantheistic symbol, with some kind of modelling analogy to the Supreme Creator. On the normal, empiric zoological level the insect was considered to be an interesting representative of nature's species, but nothing much more. But in the decades after 1800 Romanticism and its new feverish imagination created a novel literary vision of the spider, a vision that linked him with a new conception of female character and psychology in a way destined to evoke feelings of fear, sometimes even of horror. This is another story.

4 The Femme Fatale and Eroticism

A hundred years ago the German writer Hanns Heinz Ewers – known for his penchant for phantastic and occult themes, but also for his scientific interest in ants and insects – created the classic story which connected, by means of a gripping literary rendering, the spider with the peculiar thematic complex of the femme fatale.[1] The short story, entitled simply 'The Spider' (1907), is set in Paris, in a small hotel in the Montmartre district. The establishment is scarred by the fact that three unrelated, socially and psychologically different, successive occupants of one and the same hotel room have inexplicably committed suicide therein – after inhabiting it only for a week – by hanging themselves on the window catch. All three were known for their positive, optimistic attitude to life. The last one to die in such a terrible way was a robust, war-proven ex-serviceman, sent there by the police to help to discover the causes of the two earlier deaths.

Alarmed by this mysterious sequence of events, the Montmartre district police chief found a candidate seemingly endowed with the steadiest of nerves, a young student in need of a cheap lodging and with a longing in his heart for a challenge of some kind. The police equipped him with a telephone, kept contact with him and asked him to write down his observations in the form of a diary.

Soon the student spotted in a window in the house opposite the hotel a young, mysterious woman, clad in a black dress with violet dots and black handkerchiefs. She sat at the window, spinning and spinning on . . . Day after day the student became more and more fascinated, observing her almost incessantly. When he did not look at the window he tried to write down his observations, though with each passing day they appeared more and more disjointed, reflecting his mounting agitation. He paid now little attention to the outside world, but in the one rare moment when he did not look at the woman in the window he observed by chance a mating ritual of two spiders on a window placed against the inside court of the hotel, a ritual that ended – after the copulation – with the death of the male spider.

Alas, the ending was the same: the student was found hanging on the window catch, and between his teeth one could discern a gnashed black spider with violet dots. A similar spider had been observed in the room after two of the earlier three deaths, but evidently the clue had not been followed up. The frantic investigation undertaken by the police revealed only the astounding fact that the flat in the house opposite the hotel was uninhabited and had stood empty for months.

Ewers carried the myth of the spiderish femme fatale to its extreme in his story, but it is not, as horror stories go, a logical extreme. The passivity of the student has obvious masochistic traits, in itself signalizing a state of psychic regression. A structural analysis of the narrative cannot fail to uncover the ambivalence of the story's message: on the one hand the death of the spider seems to be directly linked to the earlier breaking of the (mirror) image of the woman, an image created in the feverish fantasy of the student. Conversely, we might interpret it as a revival of the Freudian principle that sexual attraction must be carried to its logical end, that is, to the mutual annihilation of the lovers. Going further, the fact that the student's room is placed between two threatening spiders – the spinning lady on the opposite side of the street, and the murderous female spider on the corridor shown in the act of killing its male sexual partner – becomes obvious only after a renewed close reading of the diary. Last but not least, Ewers makes here very precise arachnological references: the spinning lady-spider in the window with her black dress with violet dots, is none other than the stunning European widow spider, the malmignatte (*Latrodectus tredecimguttatus)*, whose bite, like that of all widows, can result in an accelerated heart rate or muscle paralysis.

Ewers's classic story must come always to mind when discussing the relation between the femme fatale and the spider. This association and its various strands go back to early modern concepts and ideas. In the sixteenth century the famous alchemist and philosopher of nature Paracelsus proposed to trace the origin of spiders to solidified menstrual blood, thus pointing towards the women's primitive erotic status – menstrual blood being perceived as signally 'unclean' and thus in a way threatening.[2] To pursue this particular strand further, it is obvious that for many males gnarled pubic hair also discloses at first sight distinct arachnoid features, thus raising different fears, of which we will only here mention the spectre of a murderous *vagina dentata.*

The connexion between love and spiders goes back to antiquity, though Socrates, who, according to Xenophon's *Memorabilia,* was the first to use it, referred not to women but to young boys when comparing the dire consequences of amorous kisses to the bite of the spider.[3] Since the beginnings of the seventeenth century the spider's web was commonly connected both in literature and in popular emblem books with the feminine art of seduction. It is in the famous Dutch moralizing emblem book by Jacob Cats (*Sinne- en minnebelden,* 1618) that a spider's web was introduced for the first time into the symbolism of love. To quote here a modern English translation of the emblem's Dutch epigram:

> It is Venus's entangling web, the web you see hanging here,
> Into which many a creature falls, but none remains ensnared
> Save a few small beasts that lack both courage and strength.
> Such, alone, are caught in Venus's web. [4]

But even in this traditional reference to the moral dangers of the art of seduction there appears, in a Latin version of the motto (*non intrandum, aut penetrandum*; either stay without or break right through) of Cats's emblem, a kind of subtle allusion, through the use of the word 'penetrandum', to coitus. In that case the spider's web would symbolize the hymen, both being weakly structured obstacles which cannot offer much resistance to determined males. Cats uses also a quotation from Montaigne that ventures, in reference to the spider's web as hymen, a rather cynical piece of advice to flimsy males: 'Le vice est de n'en pas sortir, non pas d'y entrer.' ('It is not a vice to get in, but it is reprehensible not to be able to get out'.) [5]

At the beginning of the Romantic era, this emblematic motif of erotic entrapment in a spider's web received an even sharper edge. In the *Biographies of the Insane* (1795/6), written by the then immensely popular German pre-Romantic writer Christian Heinrich Spiess, an insane person speaking about erotic dangers comes astoundingly close to the later myth of the femme fatale, though some ingrediences are still lacking: 'In the same way as the spider does, we are caught by cunning women, and when we are entangled in the web of love, they are going to torture us unto death.' [6]

Black Widow
spider with prey.

96

In a certain way the ascent of the spider-woman in the nineteenth century reflected the crisis of old family values and paternal structures. In that century the increasingly used literary device of arachnophobia merged with a real or playful fictious misogyny. Women were demonized by identifying them with various incarnations of the voracious female spider, such as the Black Widow, the tarantula or the more distantly related species of the praying mantis. The threatening spider-woman stood for an alien, eloigned creature unencumbered by family obligations and the demands of fertility. Thus she could adhere, in her role as the proverbial Black Widow, to the dechristianized, nocturnal strata of society indulging in lust and sex, even at the cost of subsequent death. The contrast to the Christian-tinged symbolism of the ant and the bee, with their adherence to family values and fertility, was of course intended.

Jacob Cats, 'non intrandum, aut penetrandum', 1618, emblem illustration.

Next of kin to the spider lady were the vampire lady, numerous women with threatening stings, and last but not least the strange, new, disturbing category of the so-called phallic women.

The Romantics had conceived the fusion of the old motif of the Devil as spider with the new motif of the devilish seductress or femme fatale. Ewers does not refer to the first, since the *fin de siècle* did not have much use for the theological Devil. But in the Swiss writer's Jeremias Gotthelf famous early novelette *Die schwarze Spinne (The Black Spider,* 1842),[7] the leitmotif of the complicated narrative is brought about by a pact with the Devil concluded by a courageous young women named Christine, who allows the Devil to kiss her lips. In the part of her lips kissed by the devil, 'black spiders are born'. It is obvious that the kissing scene constitutes only a weakly veiled metaphor for the sexual act and for Christine's subsequent pregnancy, with the Devil the

Lantern-slide of a man and woman in middle of spider web to illustrate a popular song, 'The Spider and the Fly', c. 1901.

father. The birth of the child sets off a tumultous chain of events, which cannot here be described in greater detail. We see here successive identifications of a strong woman with sexuality, the devil and the spider, the latter not only on the symbolic, but also on the literal level, since Christine will in turn become transmogrified into the black arachnoid. The spider stands however not only for the Devil, but also for the epidemic that periodically ravages the village. The epidemic is described by Gotthelf in terms resembling the vocabulary of late medieval and later witch-hunts, thus connecting the habitual demonizing of women in the Middle Ages with the more literary misogynistic practice of the nineteenth century.

The spider stood however symbolically not only for the femme fatale, but also for sexuality as such, including the inner erotic demons of males. Seen under that aspect, it plays a great role in the writings of Dostoyevsky.[8] Though we meet the spider-motif in his novels mostly in form of attributes or characterizational references and not as an independent motivic strand, we can see it as expressing important layers of the great writer's symbolic universe and ideology. Generally the spider comparison served in Dostoyevsky's novels as a symbol for a depraved and predatory male sexual urge (Dostoyevsky only used it in one novel as a characterizational element in reference to a femme fatale). Sometimes Dostoyevsky uses the spider analogue with peculiar intensity – thus Dmitry Karamazov, a protagonist of the *Brothers Karamazov*, is endowed with a multitude of arachnoid references. He is a self-proclaimed 'noxious insect' with a heart 'bitten by a spider', he is immoral and plans to sexually abuse a helpless young woman by acting like 'a venomous tarantula'. The spider analogy is used on the physiognomical level for rich and poor alike, for aristocrats – so we meet a Prince Valkovsky looking like a 'huge spider' – and for poor, downtrodden, yet

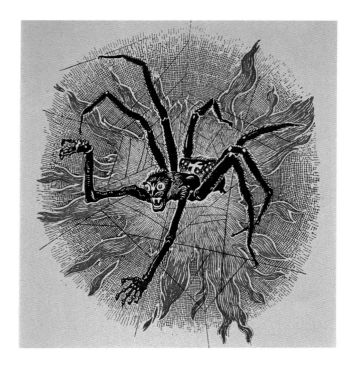

Cover-design for
a 1937 edition of
Jeremias Gotthelf's
1842 novel *Die
Schwarze Spinne
von Gottheit.*

'spiderish' prisoners. Principally it is applied to seducers, who
must feel, in the words of the hero of *Raw Youth,* that there is a
dangerous, erotic 'spider lurking in their soul'.

The heart-breaking suicide of a 12-year-old girl attended from
a distance by the culprit, the terrible Stavrogin (*The Possessed),*
who by earlier abusing her had already killed her in a spiritual
sense, is accompanied by the sight of a little red spider crouching
on a red pelargonium. Since neither we nor Stavrogin can see the
girl, and the only sound audible is the buzzing of a fly, the drama
is being relayed to us through the blending of the blood-like red
colour of the geranium with the red spider. It is a haunting, eerie

scene, in which each element, including the fly, has a symbolic function.[9] Thus the suicide of the young girl acquires a terrible, inescapable grim logic of its own with the little spider acting as a sort of symbolic catalyst. It is not thus surprising that in Svidrigailov's nauseating, yet genial vision in *Crime and Punishment*, hell is compared to a bath-house with spiders in the corners.

It is obvious that Dostoyevsky connects the spider with all sorts of evils, both sensual and moral. He used the spider-motif in his attacks against the foreign capital that streamed into Russia in the 1870s, a capital that in his words had covered Russia like a 'spider's web'. We are struck by Dostoyevsky's difficult, obnoxious but somehow prophetic modernity not only as regards here his deplorable, though in a certain sense maybe inevitable xenophobic streak – if we remember here the later imagery of communist, Nazist and other anticapitalist and anti-Semitic slogans in the twentieth century – but also in a related concept, a concept that saw in the selfish and eloigned spider living in remote corners an expression of the loneliness and alienation of modern man. In the words of one of the leading Russian literary historians of the period around 1900:

> The kingdom of the Karamazovs is a spider's kingdom. The ugly insect, sticking in its spider's web of voluptuousness, hangs above the world of the soul and reigns there. And man himself is like an insect, sometimes even a squashed one.[10]

But it is also obvious that Dostoyevsky, the coldblooded manipulator of his figures, was also a kind of spiderish writer, one who wove the tissue of his novels with an arachnoid-like supreme skill and cunning. The Soviet writer Lev Gumilevsky, who in the 1920s espoused a puritanical early Soviet morality, had no such skills. In his popular novel *Dog Alley* (1926) he tried to alert young communists to the destructive nature of sexual desire by explicitly using the imagery of a predatory spider.[11] Thus a promising young scientist is said to have become fatally entangled in the web of a greedy sexual spider that sucks his energy out of him, an energy sorely needed for the purposes of building a new society.

The none-too-subtle author makes no effort to disguise his prejudices against sexually active women: one of the book's chapters is entitled 'The Spider', while another is called 'The Spider Weaves its Web'. However there existed in Bolshevik circles in Russia a tradition linking bourgeois males with the image of 'sexual spiders' preying on young, inexperienced women from the working classes. The combination of class struggle and eroticism under the sign of the spider was propagated in *Spiders and Flies*, the brochure of the famous German socialist Wilhelm Liebknecht, which in a Russian translation of 1917 enjoyed a great popularity in revolutionary Russia. Dostoyevskian reminiscences might have played an important role in this process.

A special note was brought in by the slightly misogynistic Baudelaire, who excelled in comparing the spider as an 'ugly animal' with the female species, especially with women of an ugly or mediocre appearance. He went even further by comparing the pregnancy of a woman to a 'spiderish illness' – no doubt because of the spider-like shape of the pregnant belly.[12]

The famous French entomologist Jean-Henri Fabre (called by Victor Hugo the 'Homer of the insects'), describing in the ninth volume of his *Souvenirs Entomologiques* the 'tragic love life' of the mantis and the spider, garnished his narration with vivid descriptions of cases in which females devoured males. At the same time social theorists like the right-wing Frenchman Rémy de Gourmont, greatly admired by the quixotic Ezra Pound, or the

American sociologist Lester Ward, referred to the mating principles of spiders and to the disproportionality of arachnoid male and female bodies to illustrate the thesis that in most species, humans included, 'coition is but a prelude to death, and often love and death work their supreme act in the same instant'.[13] Describing the deadly rituals of the mantis and the spider, the misogynistic Gourmont even went so far as to make an allusion to great loving couples of the past.

By establishing the idea that in the organic order of things the female sex is primary and the male secondary, Ward and Gourmont solidified in a pseudoscientific way the romantic topos of the femme fatale and tried to give it an empirical foundation. What Ward had to say about the mating habits of the female spider could not but raise anxiety in his male readers:

> While the behaviour of the relatively gigantic female in seizing and devouring the tiny male fertilizer when he is seeking to do the only duty that he exists for, may seem remarkable and even contrary to the interests of nature, the fact of the enormous difference between the female and the male is according to the gynaecocentric hypothesis, not anomalous at all, but perfectly natural and normal.[14]

An unabashed piece of 1930s American pulp fiction brought these differing strands of the femme fatale-motif to a logical end. Jack Williamson was almost the earliest and certainly the longest-serving American science-fiction writer, and recently died, aged 98, in November 2006. His story 'The Wand of Doom' (1932), written when he was 19,[15] describes the tragic fate of one Paul Telfair, son of a biology professor who had been interested primarily in spiders. Not surprisingly his son followed in the footsteps of Little Miss Muffet and developed in consequence an 'unnatural arachnophobia'. Upon becoming a scientist himself, Paul worked on creating artificial bodies and intelligence. His young, beautiful but somewhat ethereal wife having died early in their marriage, he recreated and brought to life – with the help of 'electric wands of creation', that is, 'wands' which amplified and made real mental images (this was a popular technico-futuristic ploy in the science fiction literature of the 1930s) – her image and corpse, the latter assuming now the name of Elaine. After a period of unparalleled erotic bliss, a banal laboratory accident caused by Paul's sleepwalking – when his dream of spiders was unexpectedly taken up and realized by the 'wand' – led to a transmogrification of the beautiful Elaine into a gigantic tarantula: 'Her fair body seemed to melt . . . it thickened and swelled and became dark. Her limbs grew long and black, with dreadful swiftness; additional ones were thrust out, like pseudopods. Limbs and body were covered with a rough black hair . . . her white teeth became enormous and hideous fangs. Her limpid dark eyes grew scarlet, glowed insanely with implacable evil . . .'. In almost the same moment, Paul was turned into a common spider-male and the dreadful finale began to loom on the horizon.

Now Paul's earlier arachnophobia got a strikingly real base. Shorn of his demiurgic qualities, he became a mere menu item for his formerly submissive mate in a pseudo-erotic ritual, meeting the fate described earlier so aptly by Fabre, Gourmont and Ward: 'The gigantic spider had seized him in his jaws . . . The great fangs closed with a sickening sound upon his head . . . and his shrieks came mercifully no more.'[16] Williamson's text is one of the last where an identification of the femme fatale with the spider has been attempted; after the Second World War the use of this motif seems to have come to an end.

In the figurative arts the motif of the femme fatale played a secondary, though interesting role. The comparison of prostitution to a spider's web was common in France in the decades after 1850. The image of the – mostly clandestine – prostitute as a spider-like seductress seated in a cafe thus had its origin in colloquial comparisons, but was soon taken up by the comic press. In Paul Hadol's caricature *L'araignée du soir* (1875/6) a perky young girl, obviously overdone in her finery, with a great

'Arachne', a woman transmogrified into a spider, in Gustave Doré's 1850s illustration to Dante.

Paul Hadol,
'L'araignée du
soir', illustration
from *La Caricature*,
c. 1875–6.

geometric spider's web poised as an all too obvious attribute
behind her, waits in a cafe for her first victim.[17] The caricature
fails to grasp any spiderish, demoniac traits; involuntarily it
exudes a comic, petit-bourgeois moralizing tone.

A more *mondaine* or worldly tone was struck by the famous
Salon portrait painter James Tissot in his Parisian female figure
painting *L'Araignée* (1889).[18] But in the *Parisian Masques*, a
work by the celebrated misogynistic painter Félicien Rops, the
spider functions in a very demonstrative way as an attribute of

the deadly force of sexuality, visualizing the Parisian woman's Salome-like triumph over masculine adorators; the masques serve both as trophies and as allusions to spiderish erotic deceit and erotic subterfuge. The same message is conveyed by the naked woman that crouches in an early decorative Art Nouveau web on a postcard drawn by the known painter and designer Koloman Moser for the celebrated Viennese journal *Ver Sacrum* (1898), this being one of the first images in the long series of Viennese *fin-de-siècle* femmes fatales.

Félicien Rops, 'Masques Parisiens', frontis-piece to Félicien Champsaur, *Masques Modernes* (Paris, 1889).

A particular combination of symbols appeared in an early drawing by Aubrey Beardsley endowed with the telling title *La femme Incomprise* (1892).[19] The lady in Japanese costume is accompanied by a cat on her lap – a traditional symbol of female sexual lust – and a giant, pictographic spider placed on the upper border of the image. The obvious connection between those two symbolic attributes stresses even more strongly the *fin-de-siècle* ideas about the dangers and the destruction wrought on males by triumphing female sexuality. In the same period, marked by the peculiar atmosphere of *fin-de-siècle* eroticism, the young Austrian draughtsman Alfred Kubin, in whose work the spider motif played a great role (see chapter Six) created an allegory showing a deadly, yet somewhat caricaturesque spiderish erotic universe.[20] Kubin's drawing belonged to a greater cycle devoted to the erotic domination of women: one of

Koloman Moser, drawing for *Ver Sacrum* (Vienna, 1898).

the preceding drawings shows under the title *Deadly Sault* a
minuscule male jumping brainlessly into a gigantic vagina. All
erotic positions in the spider's web end in Kubin's eyes with a
sort of – to use an apt characterization of the great cultural
historian Mario Praz – 'erotic cannibalism' on the part of the
domineering femme fatale.

In 1907, the same year in which Ewers wrote his story, the
Russian illustrator Mstislav Dobuzhinsky created in his *Devil* a
grotesque image of a giant spider hovering in a kind of great
prison cell over a round of prisoners, the latter image borrowed
directly from Doré's and van Gogh's famous *Ronde des prison-
niers*.[21] On closer inspection the spider's head turned upside
down reveals somewhat grotesque feminine traits, implying a
different femme fatale iconography modelled on nineteenth-
century literary ideas about cruel Oriental heroines in the mould
of Salome or the goddess Astarte. The rather straightforward, if
not outright primitive message of Dobuzhinsky's spider shows

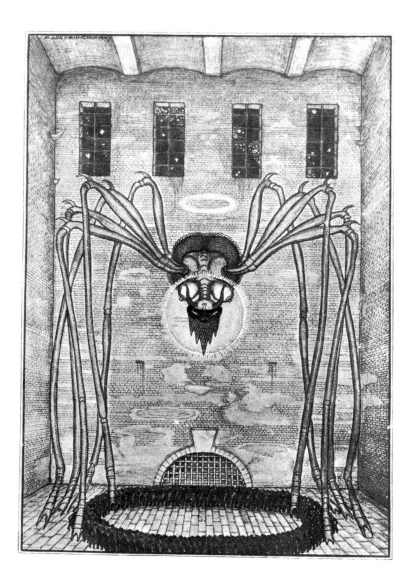

the intensity of *fin-de-siècle* misogyny, which was often to be found in circles of the extreme right.

A small classic of its own was created by the little known Austrian artist Alois Kolb with his vignette entitled *Geschlecht und Charakter* (Sex and Character) published in late 1903 in the celebrated Munich Art Nouveau journal *Jugend*.[22] The etching and its title referred to the misogynistic theses of the young Viennese thinker Otto Weininger, who had published earlier in the year a great philosophico-psychological treaty under the same title in which female sexuality and spider-like seduction techniques were described as symptoms of a civilizational crisis and as forebodings of individual death. The precocious writer was only 23 years old when he committed – three months after the publication of his treaty – an ideologically motivated suicide, despairing both of his Jewish ancestry and his repressed homosexuality. The arid, self-hating pessimism of Weininger, who despised Jews and women as corrupting agents of sexual modernity, later exerted a deep influence on Hitler (who called him 'the only decent Jew that ever existed'). In pre-war Austrian anti-Semitism the comparison of Jews to spiders and thus sexual

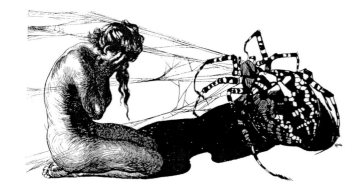

Alois Kolb, 'Sex and Character', 1903, illustration for the Munich journal *Jugend*.

112

КИНО-ДРАМА
ВЪ 5ТИ ЧАСТЯХЪ

ЗЕЛЕНЫЙ
ПАУКЪ

ВЪ ГЛАВНЫХЪ РОЛЯХЪ:
МАРІЯ РУТЦЪ
Н. М. ЦЕРЕТЕЛЛІИ } арт. Московскаго
К. П. ХОХЛОВЪ   Художест. театра.

по рис. В. Егорова
М. КАЛЬМАНСОНЪ МОСКВА

ПОСТАНОВКА А. А. ВОЛКОВА.
ДЕКОРАЦІИ Бл. Е. ЕГОРОВА.

РУССКАЯ ЗОЛОТАЯ СЕРІЯ.

РУССКАЯ ЗОЛОТАЯ СЕРІЯ

predators was especially popular and cropped up often in the publications of the Luegerites, followers of the famous right-wing mayor of Vienna Karl Lueger, who was very much admired by Hitler.

In the vignette an attractive, naked woman adopts an Eve-like attitude of regret, no doubt realizing the negative aspects of her sexuality. Her shadow, symbolizing her dark, sexual-predatory side blends on the ground into one with a gigantic black spider, who entangles her with his web. Her regrets will obviously come to naught, since the predatory dark vitalism of the spider is meant as an organic female attribute: as, what is forcibly suggested by the overlaying of the shadow, a kind of second self. Thus the spider will, being mentally the stronger, successfully overcome the woman's initial reticence and shame. It is a message very much consonant with the pessimistic theses of Weininger.

In the later Russian film poster *The Green Spider* (M. Kalmanson, J. Jegorow, 1916) Art Nouveau residues are combined with a new graphic expressivity of the black spider's shape, creating a pictographic quality that will appear in similar forms on film posters during the whole twentieth century. The reference to the green colour of the 'spider' and the wide, open eyes of the woman might refer to the metaphor of the 'green eyes of death' popular in Eastern Europe.

It may seem in some way symbolic that these utterly misogynistic images were conceived in the opening years of the twentieth century, a century destined to dramatically alter female–male relations. A century later men still refer to the spider image to describe predatory feminine sexuality, but strangely enough popular culture does not produce the relevant images any more.

5 Oppressive Mothers, Dreams and Louise Bourgeois

Though many popular books associate the psychoanalytic career of the spider with Freud, in reality the founding father of psychoanalysis had not pursued arachnoid researches of his own, but only made some approving comments on a short, but brilliant study by his Berlin follower Karl Abraham entitled *The Spider as a Dream Symbol* (1922).[1] Abraham was interested foremost in the connection of the spider to psychoses, having encountered several cases of severe arachnophobia during his psychoanalytical praxis in Berne and Berlin. The young psychoanalyst, proceeding in the footsteps of Freud, was also asked to analyse dreams of troubled patients in which spiders played a prominent part. Not surprisingly he managed to present shortly after the First World War a classic interpretation of the spider-dream and, what was more, an analysis of some important aspects of male arachnophobia. Male arachnophobia was seen by him as an expression of fear and repulsion against a domineering phallic mother. Thus Abraham constructed the psychoanalytical stereotype of a 'spiderish mother', who intends to keep her offspring forever captive in her net and tries, consciously or unconsciously, to instil in her children a permanent feeling of guilt.

A dream was described to Abraham by an extremely mother-dominated, married man in which a young servant girl – despite the young man's frantic protestations – crushes a horrid spider with a long broom in a room with two beds. According to Abraham this dream revealed the ambivalent situation of the man between his young wife in one bed (in the dream represented by the servant) and the domineering mother in the other. The energetic crushing of the spider is seen in analogy to some sadistic elements of the coitus, the long broom being thus an unmistakable phallic symbol. It reveals thus – despite the outwards protestations – the latent wish of the male to kill his spider-mother through a sort of coitus.

Another dream concerning a falling spider touching the face of a male plagued by violent castration fantasies was illustrated by the patient through a sketch showing female genitals in a spiderish form with a protruding, oblong, phallic shape in the middle. The analysed person confirmed, though not without astonishment, the suggestion of Abraham that this shape must represent a penis. The wicked mother is thus clearly endowed with a male genital organ; the shape of the spider could be interpreted as a symbol of erection. To quote Karl Abraham:

> We arrive thus at the conclusion that a second symbolic meaning can be assigned to the spider; it represents the penis embedded in the female genitals which is attributed to the mother.[2]

Abraham's pioneering paper initiated a discussion in which Freud also participated. The exchanges between Abraham, Freud and the psychoanalyst Hermann Nunberg concerned dreams where the danger of being killed by the spider-mother during incestous intercourse was expressed in a more open manner. In the fact that the spider kills its victims by sucking their blood, Nunberg preferred to see a symbolic equivalent of castration fears: that is, he saw it as an expression of stereotypical fantasies and fears of losing one's penis during the sexual act. Freud on the other hand pointed to the fact

> that the female spider is far superior in size and power to the male; during copulation the male runs a very great risk of being killed and devoured by the female. There exists therefore a striking agreement between the ideational content of the phobia analysed by Nunberg and a fact of natural science.[3]

These statements were part of an improvised exchange; however, by referring to Abraham's findings in his authoritative handbook *New Introduction to Psychoanalysis* (1933),[4] Sigmund Freud gave the spider-mother complex a sort of official psychoanalytic sanction.

Psychoanalysts following the Freudian tradition tend now to distinguish between the genital-located spider fears raised by aggressive 'castrating' mothers and the fact that the spider may represent the fear of a pregenital, namely orally incorporating mother.[5] A special symbolic aspect relates to the spider's dropline, which some arachnophobic patients belonging to the second group associate with the mother's umbilical cord.[6] The latter serves as a vehicle for the patient's oral fears of being engulfed by his mother.

Freud's great rival Carl Gustav Jung attempted also some arachnoid interpretations. Interpreting a dream in which a great, metallic UFO-like spider floated down from heaven, he ventured the explanation that it represented a paranoiac attempt at constructing an analogy to a God-like figure.[7] Jung mixed together in his explanation elements of the then fashionable UFO-fiction with the traditional devouring role of the spider and further on with old Asiatic myths associating the spider with the centre and order of the world. In Jung's analyses, the fear of being caught by a spider is tantamount to the fear of losing one's ego, because the middle point of a spider's web, by resembling the mythical centre, must automatically dissolve the essence of everybody caught into it. The victim 'will be put in the situation of the world's creator, who is everything and who has nothing outside it'.[8] These words concluded Jung's interpretation of a dream of a depressive patient in which the latter discovered in the attic of his house a great, blue cross-spider 'sparkling like a diamond'. Nonetheless Jung upheld to a certain point the traditional Freudian interpretation of the spider as the all-encompassing mother. Presenting a sophisticated dream-analysis in which a black spider was affixed with nails to a stake, subsequently changing its shape to that of a cross, Jung saw in this a symbol of transition from a maternal Marian attachment to a rational Christomorphic outlook.[9] Interestingly enough, none of the great psychoanalysts of the first generation referred expressly to the fact that the sight of gnarled, protruding pubic hair might raise associations with spiders in some males.

Among the many known modern dreams connected with the spider one should mention a dream experienced by the great Swiss sculptor Alberto Giacometti in 1921, but published only 25 years later in the famous surrealist journal *Labyrinthe*, in which two spiders, one brown and one yellow, played the central part.[10] In his dream Giacometti had first loudly demanded the killing of the brown spider, only to flee moments later in acute arachnophobic panic from his bed. Then he seemingly woke up – in reality he was still dreaming – and saw another threatening spider, this time a crustacean-like specimen of yellowish complexion. The latter spider was crushed by Giacometti's girlfriend, only to be transformed into a zoological exhibit, which had obviously been needlessly destroyed. The third encompassing dream had as its central motif Giacometti frantically trying to cover up the alleged misdeed of destroying a museum exhibit.

Awakened, Giacometti discovered on his skin a yellowish tinge, as if he was infected by the crushed spider. His girlfriend decided to touch the yellow parts of his body, laughing in the process. Some time later a close friend of his died; the description of the dead man stresses the spider-like aspect of the latter's horribly dried up, evanescent corpse.

Giacometti then tried to reconstruct his dream by providing a description of the two spiders. Contrasting the first's soft, hairy structure to the uncanny crustacean-like constitution of the second he obtained a kind of a positive–negative arachnoid symbolism which referred in an obvious way to the sequence of events. Later psychoanalysts were tempted to see in the 'soft squashy body and the projecting limbs of the spider an objectification of the soft-nauseating feelings produced after an orgasm, starting in the solar plexus and spreading out to the other parts of the abdomen and body like the legs of the spider' (J. A. Hadfield, 1969).[11] Though Giacometti's dream eschews a stringent interpretation and the erotic element is subdued, the reference to the woman-spider as the erotic element – the yellowish tinge refers to Giacometti's venereal disease – is obvious. In his sculptures Giacometti also used or alluded to the spider motif, associating it with women and their 'black libido'. The fact that he hung a spider relief (*Femme en forme d'araignée*, 1932) on a line over his bed in his atelier seems to express a part of his oneiric experiences.

Images drawn by patients in the course of the psychoanalytical treatment have an obvious and increasingly important function in modern psychotherapy and its procedures. In that particular context we would like to refer here to two drawings made by young patients of a Jungian psychotherapeutic couple (F. Seifert, R. Seifert-Helwig)[12] who were dealing with cases of complicated conflicts between possessive mothers and their frightened and immature sons.

A youthful patient, given the pseudonym 'Konrad', had drawn his mother as a gigantic spider, presented in the very act of throttling him. The image presents a curious mixture of children's art with interesting decorative elements of expressionist vintage. One of the fangs of the spider is grabbing at the genitals of the helpless young man, as if with the intention of taking over his phallus and using it for her sinister designs. The unnatural violet colour of the spider – alas not to be seen on our photograph – might refer to the violet dots of the European widow

Patient 'Konrad', drawing, around 1950.

Patient 'Martin', drawing around 1950.

spider; in any case, it drastically amplifies the atmosphere of utter helplessness and unmitigated aggression accompanying this act of matriarchal castration. In the Jungian practice of referring to archetypes, the spider becomes thus the omnipotent Great Mother.

The second drawing, also made by a troubled youth – named 'Martin' – with an oppressive mother syndrome brings a reversal of the situation. Here the oppressed son is avenged by a marabout, an African stork known for its peculiar calm and composure, who strikes the mother-spider, which is ornamented with a golden cross, with a pointed long beak. Though the Seiferts take this act at its face value, in our opinion it could be tentatively interpreted as a symbolically transferred incest wish on the part of the young man. On the other hand the marabout displays a set of virtues the youthful patient is hoping desperately to acquire during the healing process. The patient commented on his work by saying that the only thing which will remain from the evil spider will be the golden cross, a powerful symbol that might help him during his nervous recovery. Whether the patient meant this as a reference to the particular, symbolically laden type of the cross spider is however open to question.

The cases described go back in their analysing techniques to the pre-war period, though contemporary psychotherapy also tries to subsume mother-son conflicts under the image of an all-controlling spider. However nowadays these conflicts are reconstructed, analysed and resolved situationally ('played out') in the framework of both a diagrammatic 'relation model' and a symbolic model of the whole family. Thus the popular 1990s therapeutic advice book by the Wollschlägers, *Der Schwan und die Spinne*, attempts a situational reconstruction of the 'spiderish' mother's ambivalent role – that of keeping together and linking the family in a positive sense of the word and that of controlling it in the same time. The central role is played by a great spider, which is confronted with different situations played out in a family model based on a scheme of mutual relations.[13] The victimized daughter rationalizes the choice of the spider by saying about her mother that 'she wants to have everything under control and she wants to be able to grab out in all directions'.

The medium chosen to neutralize the spider is often a kind of fuzzy mesh, where the spider's fangs and threads must lose their direction and get enmeshed. Another neutralizer is provided by a black swan as a kind of living paradox, which is meant to highlight by way of analogy the intrinsic paradox of the spider-mother: at the same time it represents both the caring and the oppressive centre of the family.

The mother as spider-complex appears also in folk tales. In a Flemish folk tale an old and ugly mother sees in a magical mirror the head of an ugly spider. This spider tries to convince the old mother to kill her beautiful daughter and thus to inherit her youth and good looks. The mirror thus shows the mother's devilish alter ego and provides us with an *avant la lettre* psycho-analytical account of mother-daughter relations.

A paradoxical sequel to the complex of the spiderish mother is provided by the very popular series of giant spiders created in the 1990s and later by octogenarian artist Louise Bourgeois. Bourgeois took up the spider motif – if we discount isolated earlier explorations – in the years 1994 and 1995 first in her celebrated *Insomnia* drawings, and a short time later in her often oversized room sculptures. For Bourgeois the spider is best understood by analysing his relations to the room. The most famous of her works, the installation *Spider* (1997), is an attempt to show the dialectics of the spider's existence in rooms and 'cells', the latter concept being derived from some of her earlier works. Her spiders often display architectonic room-shaping qualities. However their physical presence is defined at best by the ambivalence of them being at the same time in the room and outside of it, an ambivalence pertaining in a certain sense to the artist's symbolic departure point. Though the work expressly refers to the mother of the artist, it was conceived, as the artist put it, as a homage to a protective mother who gained her living – when Bourgeois was still a child – in a literally arachnoid fashion by restoring old damaged tapestries. For Bourgeois the mother-spider serves thus as a wide metaphor of connection-making – as she interprets the mother-spider's web – and caring. To the question 'Why you depict your mother as spider?' Bourgeois responded with the following posthumous accolade, ascribing a common set of positive values both to her mother and spiders: 'Because my mother was my best friend, and she was deliberate, clever, patient, soothing, reasonable, dainty, subtle, indispensable, neat and useful as an *araignée*'.[14] In the meantime the spider motif has advanced to being a

Louise Bourgeois, *Spider*, c. 1997, steel sculpture.

sort of artistic trademark of Bourgeois – on her 95th birthday
in December 2006 she was labelled in leading art journals as
an 'artspider'.

There exists however an obvious chasm between the intentions of the artist and the popular reception of her spider-
works. Her subtle drawings, showing harmonious spider families
presented with stereotypal caring characteristics, are able immediately to convey her positive view of the spider-mother;
however, her large-scale sculptures, despite some endearing
traits, arouse at first sight the threatening image of gigantic
insects having just sprung away from B-grade Hollywood spider
films. That observation is even more true in regard to the *Spider*

installation, with its fear-inducing association of the spider and the cell. Thus despite the professed intention of the artist – which does not seem to have been understood by the wider art public – these works fit rather neatly into our chapter devoted to oppressive spider-mothers.

6 Spiders in Art and Caricature

The spider seems at first sight to possess no particular attraction for artists. Reduced to a tiny, disproportionate body with its wide outreaching eight legs it appears like a particularly ugly representative of nature's animal and insect world. In marked contrast to its animal creator, the spider's web as such is mostly depicted as an attractive and decorative sight, such as in a number of graphic depictions of the transformation of Arachne into a spider,[1] or the many photographs of a dewy web in a nascent sunlight.

In fifteenth-century woodcuts, the spider, surrounded by a geometrically circular web, presented a schematized pictographic shape,[2] whereas Baroque etchings show the flimsy twinkle of the web with painterly panache. The specialized entomological and flower illustrations which started to appear in the second half of the sixteenth century – to refer only to the famous engravings by Joris Hoefnagel (1592)[3] – mostly showed the spider in an anatomically correct way, though his appearance still had some pictographic traits. The spider as a symbol played an important role in Pieter Bruegel the Elder's famous *Dulle Griet/ Mad Meg* (1562, Rotterdam, now in the Museum Mayer van den Bergh). In that depiction of a giant, fiendish woman, whose relentless fury raises hell and havoc on earth, the spider came to symbolize the scheming of the Devil and the threat of death. The visual

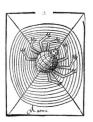

Woodcut from
Johann Cuba,
Hortus Sanitatis
(Mainz, 1491)

prominence of Bruegel's spider was caused by its exceedingly simple outline, a formal trait which went back to the tradition of a late medieval schematization.

In the seventeenth century the spider appeared in many splendid Dutch flower paintings, for example in the works of Abraham Mignon. His role as a motif in Dutch painting is not however easy to define. On the one hand his presence in flower paintings was deemed necessary as a prerequisite for achieving a measure of botanical and zoological realism. The first theoretical and historical treatise on Dutch painting, written in 1678 by Samuel van Hoogstraten, demanded that the flower painter and still-life painter should depict 'multicoloured bouquets of flowers in pots and vases, grapes, beautiful peaches and apricots

Tobias Reichel,
Spider automaton,
around 1604,
brass, Dresden,
Grünes Gewölbe.

128

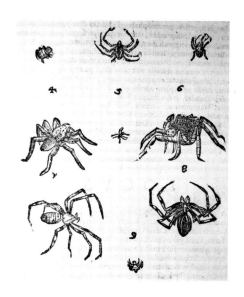

An illustration of spiders from Book v of Ulisse Aldrovandi's 1638 *De Animalibvs insectis . . .*

or melons . . . both white and coloured butterflies, lizards and spiders . . .'.[4] On the other hand, spiders were often depicted as minuscule beings, mostly hanging on a thread, prima facie looking like one of the many different insects in the painting. No visual prominence was accorded to the arachnoids, since all too often they blended almost into one with the dark background. They seem prima facie to have conveyed no particular iconographic message,[5] save some melancholic suggestions about the fragility of life. Nonetheless the possibility that they also referred to the concept of *tactus* (touch), serving thus as a symbolic rendering of one of the five senses, and that they alluded to the antonymic comparison bee–spider (as described in chapter Three) should not be excluded.

A caesura of sorts can be discerned in the years around 1700. After that, illustration cycles devoted to birds and insects

over:
A scorpion and a bird-spider on a strawberry guava, from Maria Sibylla Merian, *Metamorphosis Insectorum Surinamensium* (Amsterdam, 1705).

'MYGALE fasciée, CTÉNIZE Chasseur, EPÉIRE Militaire, LYCOSE Xyline, ERÈSE rouge' – diverse types of spiders, illustration, France, middle of the 19th century, original illustration.

1. MYGALE fasciée. | 3. EPÉIRE Militaire.
2. CTÉNIZE Chasseur. | 4. LYCOSE Xyline.
5. ÉRÈSE rouge.

J. J. Grandville, the 'Great Academy of Lagado', from his 1838 illustrations for Jonathan Swift's *Gulliver's Travels*.

included realistic and aesthetically appealing depictions of spider species. The pioneering German zoological and botanical illustrator Maria Sibylla Merian began with a style derived from the aforementioned Dutch flower bouquets, but in the years after 1700 began to render wonderfully fleshy and hairy spiders.[6] The hairy arachnoids were to remain a favourite subject of botanical illustrators in the eighteenth and nineteenth centuries, in marked contrast to the more meagre or skinny species. A broadly interpreted Merian manner seems decisively to have influenced scientific spider imagery and illustrations for almost two centuries.

The nineteenth century did not create new interesting spider images, being much more fond of the web alone. The abstract linear qualities of the web must have appealed at the onset of the century to austere classicist sentiments; its decorative

Antoine Desmoulins, *Spiders*, c. 1770s, gouache and watercolour.

133

intangibility, on the other hand, suited the later Romantic imagination. Thus we can discern an ascending line throughout the whole century as regards the imagery of the web, a line culminating, not surprisingly, in many works subscribing to the stylistics of Art Nouveau. One of the most interesting renderings of the motif was created by the great French graphic artist J. J. Grandville in his illustration (1838) of that scene from the third part of *Gulliver's Travels* in which Swift described the 'Great Academy of Lagado'. This was a topsy-turvy academic establishment where foolhardy scientists tried to invent and apply in

Hans Thoma,
The Window, 1862,
lithograph.

Tsukioka Yoshitoshi, 'Sakata Kintoki lodges in the Chambers of Minamoto no Raiko to capture the Monstrous Spider' in a scene from the Nō play *Tsuchi-Gomo*, 1885, colour woodblock print.

practice all sorts of impossible things, with 'silk from spider's threads' being high on their impossible agenda. Their concept referred however once more, though in a jocular way, to the old opposition between the spider's apparent uselessness and the silkworm's usefulness. Grandville's concentric webs are enlivened in a masterful painterly fashion, the artist succeeds in evoking the illusion of an mysterious and unfathomable web. His other images of the spider showed however a caricaturesque misogynistic touch.[7] To continue our presentation of the nineteenth century, cobwebs received a pronouncedly sympathetic treatment in the unproblematic lithography of Hans Thoma, where they stand for the values of tradition and homeliness.

It was in the period of Art Nouveau that the linear yet ornamental decorativity of the web came to suit the artistic temper of the age. Many Art Nouveau vases are decorated or totally covered with large, drawn-out webs.[8] Most of the glasses were produced by the famous French Art Nouveau glass manufactures

of Daum and Gallé, one of the extant vases bearing as inscrip-
tion the popular words of Victor Hugo about his particular love
of spiders and stinging nettles. Art Nouveau graphic webs also
invaded wooden boxes and pochettes, and such was their visual
attractiveness that we can – taken in by the beauty of the web on
the curious Swiss ex libris of 1918 – overlook at first glance the
reference to the spider's role as harbinger of death. Leafing
through the volumes of the splendid London art journal *The*

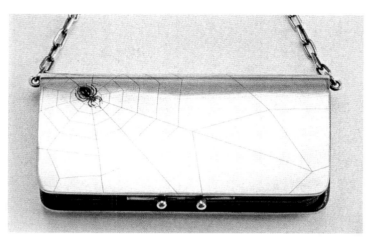

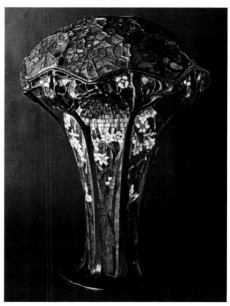

Decorative
pochette, France
or England,
c. 1910–20, silver
and enamel.

Glass and bronze
Tiffany lamp from
c. 1900.

Swiss bookplate from 1918 with skeleton-in-a-spiderweb motif.

Arthur Rackham, 'The Rescue', illustration from *The Studio*, 1906.

Ephraim Moses Lilien, illustration from Moses Rosenfeld's 1903 *Lieder des Ghetto*.

Studio, as published in the first decade of the twentieth century,[9] we are struck by the sheer multitude of spider motifs, both purely decorative and fairy-tale ones, some of them created by great book illustrators (for example Arthur Rackham).

Arachnoid motifs played an exceptional role in a magnificent German-Jewish illustrated book, *Lieder des Ghetto* (Songs of the Ghetto, 1903), which presented a German translation of

56

Auf dem Totengarten.

Die Nacht ist stille. Es leuchtet der Mond,
Es schimmern und blitzen die Sterne —
Mich trägt der Traumgott durch Leben und Tod
In mitternächtige Ferne — — —

Das ist ein großes Leichenfeld:
Da ruhen so Gute wie Schlechte,
Begrabenes Glück, begrabenes Leid,
Der Herr ruht neben dem Knechte. . .

Nur manchmal rauscht ein Weidenbaum,
Der Wind spielt in den Zweigen. . .
Sonst weit im Feld kein Laut, kein Laut,
Die Toten, die Toten, sie schweigen. . .

Viel hundert Gräber, kalt und stumm.
Ich starr' sie an beklommen.
Viel hundert Gräber — sie scheiden sich wohl —
Von Armen, Reichen und Frommen. . .

Der Wind streicht übers Leichenfeld,
Es rascheln die Blätter und Blättlein:
„Eine heilige Ruh in den Gräbern euch,
Eine heilige Ruh in den Bettlein!"

Mich packt ein Schauder. Der Traumgott spricht:
„Zur Rechten und Linken die Steine,

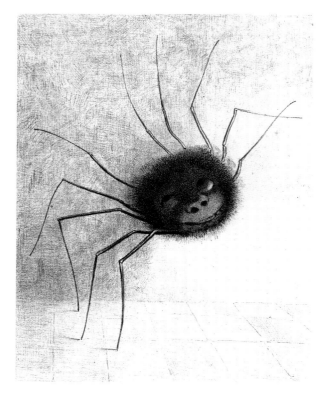

Odilon Redon,
Smiling Spider,
1887, lithograph.

the poems by the American-Yiddish writer Morris Rosenfeld[10]
together with excellent illustrations by the renowned Jewish
artist Ephraim Moses Lilien. Despite its attractive shape relating
to Art Nouveau decorativity, the spider's web – symbolically
covering both the views of poor Jewish workshops and those of
the shtetls – exudes a sharp-edged, proto-expressionist feeling
of uneasiness. It stands here for civilizational distance, for the
strictures of Jewish provincial life, for the lack of modernity, for
the all-pervading, gloomy atmosphere of the ghetto. A leitmotif

Ephraim Moses
Lilien, another
illustration from
Rosenfeld's *Lieder
des Ghetto*.

of sorts is provided by the recurrent border-image of the cross-spider – an all too obvious symbolic allusion to Christian anti-Semitism – gnawing mercilessly at the poor Jewish heart.

Some interpretational difficulties arise in the case of the two popular lithographs by Odilon Redon, showing the *Smiling* and the *Crying Spider*.[11] Those lithographs, created in the year 1881, display at first glance strong caricatural traits. Yet the *Crying Spider*, alluding to St John the Baptist, its head resting on the body like John's on the salver, might depict an image of the mental anguish experienced by the artist himself. Maybe Redon intended a veiled autobiographic reference – in the vein of the contemporary analogy by the great writer and historian Jules Michelet of the spider with the artist who, faced with the absence of his 'canvas', finds his confidence gone.[12] Redon's impressive *Smiling Spider* demonstrates a semi-grotesque friendly puckishness of sorts.

A private letter by Redon written in 1876 to his wife Camille[13] relates the story of a spider he found on his red bolster, which he subsequently befriended and placed on his wall to watch 'her' progress over his paintings and drawings. Finally he even associated the spider with his beloved. Redon might have remembered here Michelet's vivid description of the love life of spiders as the 'dark romances of our ceilings' ('noirs amours de nos plafonds'). On the other hand Redon had very difficult relations with his mother and with women in general, which might, to refer here to Abraham's Freudian arachnoidal psychoanalysis, help to explain the spider motif.

The spider was and is a potent caricatural image, functioning primarily as a symbol of political dominance and oppression.[14] A German single-leaf print from the first phase of the Thirty Years War (1621) shows a great spider's web spread out over a small hill.[15] The web holds captive symbolic models of cities

Odilon Redon, *Crying Spider*, c. 1881, charcoal drawing.

143

Thomas
Rowlandson,
'THE CORSICAN
SPIDER IN HIS
WEB', 1808,
hand-coloured
etching.

taken by Catholic armies after the Battle of the White Mountain (1620), the spider on the hill below continues the acts of aggression by attacking a number of heraldic animals, representing the particular princes and territories of the beleaguered Protestant coalition. The spider as such is an obvious – though etymologically incorrect – allusion to the name of the then prominent Hapsburg Catholic military commander Spinola.

A classic version of the motif of the spider-oppressor was published in 1808 in England, created by the known caricaturist Thomas Rowlandson. In the centre of the gigantic web we see Napoleon's characteristic profile – the Emperor was then at the apogee of his power. In his web captive flies represent the countries and rulers of Europe defeated or occupied by the French. Only the British fly hovering in the uppermost part proclaims defiantly that she will not allow herself to be caught. Five years later (1813), in a new political and military situation,

'Neue Wahrheit',
Germany, 1621,
single-leaf print:
the Catholic
spider attacking
Protestant
territories.

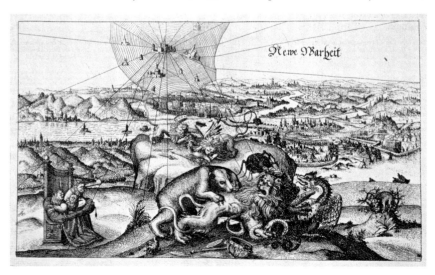

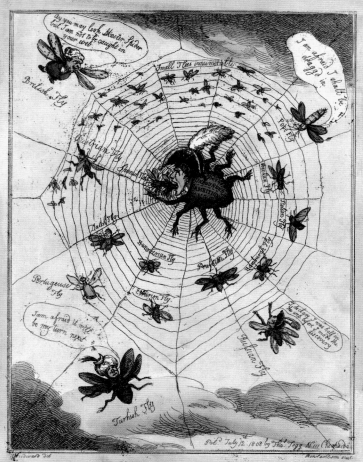

THE CORSICAN SPIDER
IN
HIS WEB!

a German caricature commented on Napoleon's string of defeats by showing the profile of the emperor with a spider's web on his breast carrying the names of cities and of battles lost now by Napoleon's armies, in the act of being swept away by an alien hand.

After Rowlandson's caricature, the spider's web functioned as an image of oppressive political control from one dictatorial centre. However, the idea that the monarch should, like the spider, be at the centre of the web of government was not necessarily a sign of the monarch's aggression, as we tried to show earlier, since it equated the spider's web with an administrative and an information network. From a dozen or more nineteenth-century caricatures of different spider-like rulers and politicians (for example Charles x or Napoleon iii)[16] we have chosen here the image of Tsar Nicholas i as the 'Spider of the North', drawn during the Crimean War by the great French illustrator Gustave Doré (1854) as a part of his acerbic *Histoire de la Sainte Russie.*[17] The web around Tsar Nicholas is constructed from the false slogans and empty promises of this dictatorial monarch.

A slightly different message is conveyed by the anti-commune French lithograph of 1872 portraying the young French communard Théo Ferré with a small, but threatening spider on his forehead. Ferré, a radical revolutionary, served in the police in the last bloody last month of the Paris Commune, being responsible for many arrests and the famous execution of hostages, which included an archbishop. He was tried in September 1871 and executed forthwith; the caricature thus serves as a posthumous defamation. The spider shown here represents the oppressive bloodthirstiness of the police. In a crafty physiognomic man-animal analogization, Ferré's facial traits were imprinted with a 'spiderish' allure. A similar analogization turned into a scheme is to be found on anti-Semitic postcards, which not

Gustave Doré, Tsar Nicholas i as the 'Spider of the North', 1854, woodcut.

146

only associated Jewish facial traits with those of 'bloodsucking spiders', but also showed them with with long, grabbing, spider-ish hands.

This depressing genre enjoyed its greatest popularity in Russia around and after 1900 – where it echoed the anti-Semitic slogans of the Russian nationalistic and religious Right about depraved and bloodthirsty Jewish spiders 'catching by subterfuge innocent Russian flies' – and of course later under the Nazis.[18] In a public triumphal march in the venerable German university town of Tübingen in 1936, undertaken with the aim of celebrating anti-Jewish legislation, local Nazis set up a sort of carnivalesque chariot on which a great papier-maché figure showed a grotesque Jewish head with a spiderlike body and long spiderlike fangs.

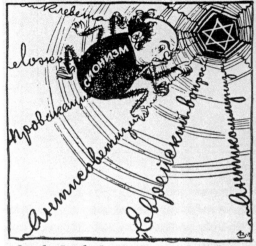

Anti-Semitic Soviet
caricature, 1971.

Anti-Semitic
Russian nationalist
caricature, 1992.

In the 1930s many antifascist artists tried their hand at a Nazi-web with a central swastika (for example John Heartfield, 1935). A poster by the Bavarian Social Democrats had appealed earlier (1929) to the Bavarian electorate in order to tear apart the then nascent Nazi web – alas without real success. Contemporary caricatures readily use the spider's web as a political motif: among hundreds of examples let us mention here a 1990 caricature by Walter Hanel showing the reunification of Germany being overshadowed by the sinister legacy of the East German secret police, the famous Stasi. But of course the scheme of the domineering spider could be used also for more mundane, unpolitical subjects, for example in John Tenniel's famous *Punch* caricature (1868) making fun of turf mania, or a variation by Linley Sambourne, which appeared eight years later also in *Punch*, ridiculing the new enthusiasm for tennis.

The Jewish conspiracy to rule the world in an anti-Semitic postcard, c. 1930.

'Tear up the web, vote for the Social Democrats!', anti-Nazi poster in Bavaria, 1929.

Anti-Nazi woodcut,
Hans Gerner,
Stuttgart,
around 1930.

Two interesting images were without the web, one the gro-
tesquely primitive West German anti-Stalinist poster of 1951
showing Stalin as a monstrous spider in the act of preying on
the youth of Western Europe. Another, earlier and artistically
much better, negative spider image succeeded in fusing the
folk-art tradition of the Mexican cult of death with a gripping
piece of political polemics. In 1913 the great Mexican artist José
Guadelupe Posada portrayed the Mexican President Huerta as
a *Calavera Huertista* (The Huertist Skeleton).[19] The cruel, strong-
arm politician Huerta is depicted here as a revolting hairy spider,
crawling with maggots and holding the bones of his victims.

Posada created a stunning overall design, balanced, but at the same time expressive, with an obvious focus on the predatory skull of Huerta. The latter is reported to have become so incensed at Posada's temerity that he ordered the printing house razed on the spot. Posada's wonderful zinc engraving is perhaps the best example of the iconographic identification of the spider with death. In its most popular form the motif – known since the seventeenth century – presents a spider crawling on a skull. This message might also be seen as a variation of the former identification of the spider with heresy.

John Tenniel,
'The Turf Spider
and the Flies',
from *Punch* (1868).

STALIN SUCHT SOLDATEN
AGENTEN UND SABOTEURE!
Kommunistische
Weltjugendfestspiele
JUGEND ABER WILL FREIHEIT!
Darum mit uns!
BUND DEUTSCHER JUGEND

José Guadelupe
Posada, *Calavera
Huertista*, 1913,
zinc engraving.

Around 1900 the post-Romantic negative spider myth reached its peak, producing gigantic and grotesque threatening spiders symbolic of death, the Devil and many other sorts of evil. In Théophile Steinlen's polemical lithograph from 1902, which constitutes a sort of vitriolic commentary on the completion of the famous votive Basilique du Sacré-Coeur on the Montmartre hill, the allegory of political Catholicism in France takes on a mongrel spiderlike shape with skeleton-like hands. Steinlen's stridently anticlerical tone refers to the very apogee of the conflicts between church and state in France in the first decade of the twentieth century. The German cartoonist A. Paul Weber produced in the decades before 1980 a number of devilish skele-

West Germany,
Stalin as a spider
threatening the
youth of Europe,
1951 poster.

Théophile Steinlen,
The Church,
an anti-clerical
allegory incor-
porating Paris's
Sacré-Coeur, 1902,
lithograph.

tal spider images in the vein of Steinlen, conceived as general allegories of German *Angst.*

A related sequence of spider images and caricatures, drawn by a number of European artists in the very first years of the twentieth century, took as its point of departure the figure of a giant spider, incorporating to a varying degree references to the iconography of death and the Devil. However the main visual accents were provided here by the prophetic – when we consider for example the much later development of popular sci-fi- and horror film imagery – effects of depicting the spider on a dispro- portionately large scale. In Alfred Kubin's *Epidemic* (1902) a giant spider-like death is sowing the germs of illness and death; in Bruno Paul's *Epidemy in South Africa* a giant spider, accompanied by rats, creates a panic among the population; another drawing from these years showed a similar, spiderish

Martian Man in the act of provoking the panicky flight of onlookers.[20] Dobuzhinsky's *Devil*, discussed earlier, belongs at first sight to the same out of scale spider-image series of the *fin de siècle*, though somewhat untypically it made direct reference to the motif of the femme fatale.

The visual scheme of the disproportionate spider might present an appellative visual directness, but in artistic terms it was an obvious failure. The best artistic results were achieved – Kubin's other excellent spider drawings testify to that effect –

Bruno Paul, the Boer War in South Africa seen as a spider-driven outbreak of plague in a cartoon from *Simplicissimus*, 1902.

when the effects are somewhat reduced, and when a twilight atmosphere suggests some undefined threat. The difference becomes obvious when contrasting Kubin's cover of the treatise *Die Schöpfer* (1920) written by the mystic philosopher Salomo Friedländer (pseudonym Mynona), where the ugliness of the spider evokes a surreal feeling, with the primitive expressivity of an anonymous 1937 Swiss cover of the book edition of Gotthelf's *Black Spider*.

Alfred Kubin,
cover-design
for 'Mynona',
Der Schöpfer
(Munich, 1920).

François
Delarozière,
La Princesse
on location in
Liverpool, 2008.

After Art Nouveau and Kubin the spider-motif did not occupy modern artists to a comparable degree – at least until the 1990s, when the spiders of Louise Bourgeois (see chapter Five) claimed universal attention. Nonetheless Bourgeois owes much to the proto- and surrealist phase of Alberto Giacometti in which he explored the positioning of spiderlike forms in space, as in his flattish relief *Femme en forme d'araignée* (1932) which the artist placed hanging on the line over his bed in his atelier and documented in a famous drawing.[21] Not surprisingly the spider also interested Alexander Calder (*Spider*, 1940, MOMA) and the French sculptress Germaine Richier (a number of sketches and sculptures between 1946–73),[22] who were both influenced by Giacometti. In each of the attempts the exploration of the surrounding space played an important role. This is even more true of the giant fifty-foot mechanical spider (*La Princesse*) projected by François Delarozière and executed by the French *La Machine* group, which was put up at different locations in Liverpool in 2008. In 2009 *La Princesse*, together with a new mechanical

Moche culture,
Peru (gold bead
with spider,
c. AD 300).

spider named *Lady*, went on to Yokohama. Whereas the Yokohama officials prefer to stress the fact that spiders as such stand
for 'networking', and thus can express the spirit of a great har-
bour city like Yokohama, linked commercially with the whole
world (a similar rationale could also be claimed by Liverpool),
the countless press reports suggest a less than intellectual and
more Disneyland-like reception of the spiders by the urban
public. One can see in these novel 'spider machines' a new type
of mobile public art intent on blurring the boundaries between
high and low art, and one which (at least as regards the first
Liverpool locations) evidently had profited from the model of
the spatial arrangements of Louise Bourgeois's *Spiders* (for
example in the Tate Modern) and even more so from the visual
stereotypes of Hollywood spider B-movies, or Barry Sonnenfeld's
'steampunk' film *Wild Wild West* (1999). Despite the sombre

A spider-design in the famous 'Nazca lines', Peru.

public mood reflecting the economic crisis, this piece of extra-vagant, jocular, public design seems to have been enthusiastic-ally accepted by both the English and the Japanese publics.

Something has to be said here also about representations of the spider in prehistoric and primitive non-European societies. The question of the oldest extant spider image recently received a new turn, on the basis of finds produced by the excavations in Göbekli-Tepe (near Urfa in south-eastern Anatolia) conducted since 1995 by the German archeologist Klaus Schmidt. In an abandoned sanctuary site, which he convincingly proposed to date to the years 9000–8500 BC, Schmidt found among other animal images a pictogram of a spider.[23] Three thousand years later, the inhabitants of another Anatolian cultic place related to the pioneering Göbekli Tepe culture used a spiderlike image of a six-legged zigzag creature with a triangular head as a decoration of seals guarding their treasures, thus commencing an association of the spider with the guardianship of a hoard or treasure, an idea which is even today to be found in Hollywood films.

Stylized spiders played an exceedingly important role in the so called Moche culture (AD 100–800) in Peru. The spider – considered a powerful figure, even serving as a godlike symbol of decapitation – appeared there in a variety of forms, as on a necklace composed of beads showing a circular spider's web with the body in the form of a human head and assuming a Medusa-like expression. Arachnoid motifs in the Moche culture also appeared on figure pots. Needless to say a spider turns up also among the famous Peruvian Nazca lines dug out in the desert at the beginning of the first millennium. A later example of Pre-Columbian spiders can be found in Costa Rican indigenous

Costa Rican
spider pendant.

cultures in the form of an elaborate golden pendant. In the post-Columbian Indian cultures in Mississippi and Illinois, where a so called Southern Death Cult (1550–1700) with a penchant for spider images closely reflected Pre-Columbian ideas and mythology,[24] we can find many simplified stylizations of the spider placed on gorgets functioning probably as protective amulets.

7 Myth and Folklore

If we take the myths connected with cosmogony and the genesis of the human race as our point of departure, then the particular importance of the spider in the pertinent African and Indian myths soon becomes apparent.[1] Certainly our arachnid played a much bigger mythico-symbolic role in these parts of the world than in the mainstay of the Western tradition, a tradition that had originated with the Hebrew Old Testament and Greek philosophy. To start with, in around a dozen of these myths or narratives there appeared a kind of primordial spider either credited outright with creating the world or portrayed at least as an important collaborator in the task of creating and furbishing the human living space. All of these myths refer in the first place to the weaving faculties of the spider, seeing in the web either an instrument of the creation of the world creation or a paragon of the cosmological processes.

Perhaps the most popular mythogenic narrative has been created in West Africa, with a particular centre on the so called Gold Coast, among the Ashanti tribes, though some sources mention also the powerful Hausa tribes. Later these stories spread through Africa,[2] subsequently also reaching the Caribbean islands.[3] Many African tribes believed in the spider hero Anansi or Ananse, who seems close to the category of a Proteus-like hero. In some tales Anansi takes up the role of the demiurgic God Creator, a God who has created the sky and the stars but who also has woven the substance from which all men are issued. In the greater part of these mythical tales Anansi does these works at the behest of his father, the sky god Nyame.

Anansi is sometimes portrayed as a Prometheus-like benefactor and teacher of mankind (the Cherokee Indians also link the spider to mankind's knowledge of the sun and fire). Partly god, partly human, Anansi taught men the principles of agriculture, and is also among some tribes held responsible for causing the much needed rainfall. In one popular story Anansi decided to gather in one place all the world's wisdom and to shut it up in a sort of box. Then however he came to realize the pointlessness of his endeavour, since he himself could not carry the heavy weight of the world's collected acumen. This tale is certainly in some way connected with the saying of the West African Akam tribe: 'The wisdom of the spider is greater than that of all the world together.'

Let us mention some other myths bestowing on the spider the role of a primordial god: in Mali a great spider-god created the stars and the day/night alternation; in Cameroon he goes under the name Nyiko and is the son of the supreme god;[4] in Micronesia the creation of the world is ascribed to one god, who however functions under the two entities of the Old and Young Spider. Both in the Gilbert Islands[5] and among the Kayan in central Borneo there existed in the beginning a Sir Spider, in whose web a stone fell, becoming in the process the original land. Then a worm grew earth on which a tree took root, procreating in its branches the human race. There are a number of variations of this tale, with a particularly interesting one on the island of Nauru, with an ancient spider named Aerop-Enap. The Nauru mythic tale relates that in the beginning there existed

over:
Utagawa Kuninaga, Minamoto no Raiko and a giant spider, from an 1829 woodblock print triptych showing heroes battling demons.

only Aerop-Enap and the boundless sea. Thanks to his intelligence and creative faculties the Ancient Spider created other parts of the universe like the sun, the moon and last but not least man. He did it by skilfully using or motivating other creatures like the snail and the worm.

Hopi tarantula.

In the mythology of the Native Americans, the spider has created nature through weaving. Especially the Pueblo and Navajo people believe that the Great Spider Woman preceded everything on earth, glowing brightly in the primordial darkness. This Spider Creatrix moulded people from the clay of the earth, and attached herself to them by means of a thread. Many Native Americans still believe that the great Spider lives somewhere in the Spider Rock in the Navajo land and might interfere in their daily doings; their children are warned that she might punish their misbehaviour by taking them up on her web to her cavernous mountain lair. Some ethnographers think that Northern American concepts of the Great Spider woman are connected with Mesoamerican myths from Mexico. In Teotihuacán we see early murals dating from the first centuries of our era showing a spider woman who functions – according to recent investigations – as a Goddess of the Earth, of the Netherworld, of water and is thought to personify thus the process of creation.[6] But African tribes, like the Bacoco, Basa and Duala people of Cameroon, also adore the spider as their Great Mother. A child that had the misfortune inadvertently to kill a spider is commonly reprobated with the following words: 'Oh wretched! You have killed your mother.'

The Hindu spider-creator.

The great spider is not always actively engaged in the process of creation: the Bhagavad-Gita in India analogized the great Creator with the spider since he both creates and rests immovable in the centre, the Mundaka Upanishad stating that

A 1970s Mexican wooden dance-mask showing a spider covering the dancer's face.

'as the spider sets out his threads but is also able to contract them, so the world is derived from the Immortal (Brahman)'.[7]

In countless tales the spider connects with his threads the sky and the earth, acting as guardian of the sky or of the paradise therein, but also allowing God or lesser deities to reach the earth by means of the thread. The Aztec god Tezcatlipoca used a spider's thread to lower himself from the sky and to defeat his adversary, the ruler of the Toltecs. It seems very probable that he assumed the shape of the spider in the process.

The Native American Pomo tribe believe that the spider plays a St Peter-like role as regards the question of allowing somebody to enter heaven. The Native Americans of the Clear Lake district near San Francisco, the Central American Chibcha tribes and the North American Teton tribes associate the spider with the wanderings of souls. There are also a number of myths both in

Africa and among the Native Americans crediting the spider's web with providing a model of a functional order for the world. The Pima tribe believed in the same vein that the web helps to stabilize the world.

However many myths do not ascribe to the spider such demiurgic or semidemiurgic qualities. The abovementioned Anansi functions in other West African myths and tales as both a spider and a man and some of his exploits have a decidedly tricksterish quality. He wins battles with stronger enemies; he can feign his own death. He changes his status from man to spider when threatened, since he can flee high up the walls or hide himself in corners. He cheats when selling food on the market (for example, sucking out eggs through their shell but selling them as normal eggs) and is wont to play a number of competitive tricks, since he is much more clever than his adversaries. Anansi is not the only spider trickster: the Hopi recount the case of a great Tarantula, living in a cave. When she saw a young warrior in his wonderful armour she got very envious, succeeding by subterfuge in snatching it, and disappeared subsequently in the recesses of the mountain . . .

However there are also many Indian tales that highlight the cruel aspects of the Great Female Spider and which might be considered – to an extent – as prefigurations of the European topos of the spider as femme fatale. Indian tribes on the Great Plain believed in a big, fiendish ogre-like Spider which laid out traps for hunters or even went so far as to poison their meals. Then Spider attacked them, decapitated her victims and hung up their heads in her cave, with the brain taken out and drying out in the sun. The entrails she threw as a repast for the fishes in the water. Navajo tribal tales also described a giant spider net, holding human heads and bones in a kind of triumphal display. Let us close this particular strand by referring to Japanese

Dakota Native American shield.

myths which relate the particular case of a lovely Spider Goddess who sent her suitors to a certain death by giving them dangerous tasks.

SPIDERS IN EUROPEAN FOLK MYTHOLOGY

Despite appearances the spider does not play – if we compare it with Africa or America – a very prominent role in European folk tales. Nonetheless a number of tales or strands is worth mentioning. One of the most known is the association of the spider with cave topoi. In many countries we encounter tales describing how a hero on the run, pursued by bloodthirsty enemies, took shelter in a nearby cave. A spider web woven in a matter of minutes across the entrance of the cave convinced the pursuers that the targeted person was not there. To the list of the more known examples belong David fleeing from the wrath of Saul, the Polish king Wladyslaw Lokietek, the Hungarian King Bela or St Felix of Nola.

There are some notable variations: in Scotland pretender to the crown Robert the Bruce hid himself for three months in a cave. The observation of the incessant attempts of the spider to weave, despite occasional falls, his web, inspired Robert Bruce to pursue – despite many a setback – his aim of attaining the Scottish throne. A slightly different variant was elaborated by later Christian folk tales. These narratives tell us that the young Christ, threatened physically by a group of Jewish children, hid in a cave. There he moulded a spider out of clay, gave him life, and commanded him to fashion a dense web at the entrance of the cave which would protect its innermost parts from being seen by his enemies. This fabulous, obviously anti-Semitic tale was also used to explain the the genesis of the cross sign on the body of the cross-spider. However in at least one tale a spider

Hans Burgkmair the Elder, woodcut of St Conrad, left, holding a chalice with a spider (with the Virgin and St Pelagius), 1499, hand-coloured woodcut.

170

S. Conradus. 1499 S. Pelagius.

was accused of trying to suffocate the infant Christ by sealing his mouth with a web.

A South German hagiographic legend had it that during a Mass celebrated by St Conrad of Constance a spider fell into the chalice, which he held in his hand. However Conrad without hesitation drank the eucharist wine together with the spider. Some time later the living spider crawled out of the mouth of the saint, leaving the latter also unharmed. In consequence a chalice and a large spider therein habitually constitute an attribute of St Conrad.

European folk tales about the spider reflect different archetypal and didactic strands. Some tales place the spider in a decidedly negative, if not altogether demoniac role. A good example is the Estonian folk tale about the quarrel between the spider and the fly concerning conflicting claims of primacy (as to who first had woken up the sleeping wind, and so on). Another Estonian folk tale about the spider recounts us the theft of the fire – despite it being guarded by the devil – a theft commited by the crafty spider who took advantage of the fact that the tired devil had fallen asleep. Then the tired spider himself fell asleep and the fire was stolen from him by a swallow or, as a variant of the story had it, purloined by a fly. On the other hand, in a further Baltic folk tale – this time however from Latvia – the spider loses its Promethean role and is described outright as a liar and a persistent informer.

However some Baltic folk tales refer to the spider as a judicious person whom God esteemed and rewarded by allowing him to leave the sky by abseiling on the web. However his facility to commute between heaven and earth can also assume a decidedly negative connotation. A Bulgarian folk-tale reports that God, after creating the world, put down an uprising by revolted spirits. The spirits dispersed: some of them hid themselves in the water, some of them on the earth and one of them stayed hung up between earth and heaven, thus becoming a spider. The spider is obviously associated here with devilish traits.

In all these legends, myths and European folk-tales the spider appears as a woman, continuing the Hellenic Arachne tradition. There are however some languages in which the spider is masculine, as in the Slavic languages or in Romanian. A Romanian folk-tale relates the case of two children of a poor woman. When the latter was dying, only the daughter returned and cared for her and was duly rewarded by being transformed into an industrious bee beloved by everybody, who produced wax for the great church candles. The ungrateful son became a spider, selfish, isolated, living in remote, dark corners. Once more there appears here the curious antonymic pair bee – spider.

THE SPIDER IN RITUAL AND IN FOLK MEDICINE

Insofar as he was imbued with negative or even devilish traits the spider has been associated by some writers with illness and plague. Plutarch thought that the appearance of massive spider webs signalled the coming of the plague. However there seems to be only one concrete case in which the appearance of the plague was linked with spiders –according to a legend from the Lower Rhine territories the population of a whole village was annihilated by the 'plague spider'. Even stronger fears were evoked by the association of the spider with mental illness and damage to the brain. Popular sayings associate mental malfunctions with the spider and his doings. We have mentioned this line of association already when analysing Michelangelo's and Baudelaire's imagery in chapter Three. Let us refer here only to Anglo, German and French idioms – *cobwebbery, to get cobwebs in one's brain, er spinnt* (he fantasizes), *er spintisiert, er leidet unter*

Hirngespinsten (he suffers fom delusions), *avoir une araignée au plafond* (to have a spider under the cranium). Besides obvious references to mental problems these idioms refer also to more current delusional states between fantastic pretensions and straightforward ruminations. Another train of comparison rests on the fact that the mentally sick person living in the restricted world of his obsessive thoughts displays a certain affinity to the restricted existence of the spider in his own web.

An interesting tradition concerns the use of spiders in popular and magic medicine. In antiquity a spider attached to the skin was thought to help against fever. Tyrolian folk medicine combated fever by means of a spider inserted into a nutshell with small openings. After carrying it for nine days – during which the spider succeeded in 'sucking out all the venom' from the body of the sick person – the nutshell cum spider had to be thrown into a river. A similar procedure was followed in the case of maladies of the uterus, particularly keeping in mind the particularities of the female association with spiders.

Fever was also combated by swallowing a spider. In the German Lower Alps region the sick were advised to swallow between three and nine spiders in the morning, before breakfast. In a softened version of this gruesome procedure they were advised to insert the spider into a plum and thus to render it more palatable than in its natural state. The spider's task was to 'eat up the fever', the plum being reputed to work towards the same effect. The spider's web was thought also to function as a palliative of fever. In Bohemia the web was put into a head scarf and wrapped around the head, in the French Auvergne and among the Indians the spiders were rolled into small balls and then devoured. The Transsylvanian Gypsies, when afflicted by thyroid complaints, caught a cross-spider and had him smoked in a box for 7 days, devouring him in the period just after full moon. Compliance with these magical practices was thought to guarantee a speedy recovery.

Spiders were often used in cases of illnesses and deficiences of the sight, since the spider was thought to have excellent, penetrating eyes and could thus transmute these traits to the afflicted person. In Sussex failing sight was cured by devouring a spider wrapped in butter. A cross-spider placed on an eye was thought to cure styes; other eye afflictions were combated by placing a spider into a nutshell and carrying it on one's back, as in Germany's Principality of Reuss. Healing functions were also ascribed to spider eggs still ensconced in cocoons, which were blown onto the afflicted eye. A longer list of other maladies and ailments like nosebleeds, rheumatism or toothaches were also cured by a respective placing of spiders, to whom substitutive functions were ascribed. Thus in Norfolk a great spider was hung up over the bed of a child afflicted by whooping cough. A magic formula was then spoken and the spider moved on and affixed to the oven. When his carcass was totally dried up, the child had been successfully cured. On the other hand the very old and popular practice of healing wounds by means of an affixed spider web did have, as we now know very well, an intuitively rational basis. The protein structure of the web prevents it from getting mouldy, it posesses excellent antiseptic qualities and readily absorbs blood.

In many cultures the spider not only helped to cure maladies but also brought good luck by his mere presence. He guarded the house against witches, maladies and last but not least against lightning – the latter never managed to destroy a spider's web! Often the appearance of a spider signifies luck and good fortune, therefore he should not be killed under any circumstances imaginable: 'If you wish to love and thrive, let a spider run alive.' In France and Germany to spot a spider in the morning means trouble, on the other hand a spider seen in the evening signifies good luck: 'Matin chagrin, soir espoir.'

Last but not least spider images and symbolic requisites show eminent apotropaic qualities. In China the spider belongs to the 'Five poisonous animals' whose images repell evil forces and designs. Native American imitations of a spider's web executed in little corals were created with the aim to mystify the enemy. A still popular symbolic device are the Native American so-called 'dreamcatchers'. A coral web hung above a bed serves to deflect bad dreams, a hole left in the middle of the web allows the passage of good dreams.

8 Urban Legends

The contemporary global village is characterized by the spontaneous growth of so-called urban legends or mythologies. One of the classic renditions of these legends has been provided by the books of the eminent German anthropologist Rolf Wilhelm Brednich. The most important of them, published in 1990 bears the title *The Spider in the Yucca-Palm Tree: Modern Legends* and recounts in its title-tale the story of a tarantula nest found in an imported exotic Yucca palm, which a lady in Basle had received as a gift.[1] The story is based on information received from her sister, hearsay being a typical ingredient of the genre of urban legends. When watering the Yucca the Basle lady heard a strange squeaking noise. After a while she contacted a botanist who discovered in the palm a dangerous and poisonous spider species. This tale obviously suggests that exotic objects imported into Europe might be, despite appearances, very dangerous. The cover of Brednich's book displays a particular mixture of modern urban mythologems – the Yucca palm being obviously endowed with female erotic symbols.

There exist fabulous stories about spiders being powerful enough to spit poison from a distance of almost three metres, the poison in question being able to kill a man through mere contact with the human skin. A 1994 legend describes in much

The tarantula, a favourite spider-species for urban legends.

detail the strange and horrifying case of a cactus brought from Mexico.[2] Planted in a garden, it started after a while to shake. A botanist was called, realized the gravity of the situation and immediately called the fire brigade. One of them, clad in protective vestments, set the cactus on fire. After it had burnt down many dead tarantulas appeared, each almost 15 cm in diameter. The botanist explained that the tarantula spider often places its eggs in cacti. When they have all grown up, the cactus 'explodes' from within and around 150 live tarantulas are then dispersed in the vicinity.

Needless to say there exist many stories about spiders in banana crates or among other exotic vegetables imported to the northern hemisphere, to mention only the story about Black Widows in wine grapes. Some of them might reflect real situations, like the one we mentioned earlier about Australian spiders in Japanese Osaka, most are no doubt utterly imaginary.

An image from Anneka James's *Arachnophobia* project, based on the urban myth that everyone eats eight spiders in their lifetime when asleep.

However in themselves they display a particular mixture of projections into the future of our civilization, when processes of globalization and climate change as such will generate manifold insect and animal migrations, and reflect widespread Western feelings of guilt for importing cheaply exotic fruits from impoverished Third World countries. Sometimes, as already mentioned, these stories have a real base, to refer only to the criminal action of two Hungarians who attempted in 1999 to smuggle fifty tarantulas into Germany.

These stories also illustrate the particular paradox that human interference in nature mostly helps spiders. In Guam all of the twelve bird species which inhabited this Pacific isle have been exterminated by a new imported brown otter snake species. As a result the spiders, no longer threatened by birds or geckos, have taken over the tropical forests, which are now often covered by great sheet webs. Some futurologists even think that spiders might easily survive an eventual atomic catastrophe.

There exists a whole array of utterly fantastic stories which are repeated in ever more variations. Let us name here a few: each person reportedly swallows in their sleep through their open mouth up to eight spiders a year; tarantulas are hidden in cigarette machines; their eggs are to be found in chewing gum, and so on. An archetypal story concerns a young couple in Montreal who had decided to hold their marriage ceremony in a botanical garden. During the nuptials a tarantula crept up under the wedding gown and killed the young bride by its bite. Needless to say this utterly imaginary story uses the motif of death during a wedding, a traditional motif in itself, which frequently appears in different mythological accounts.

Edible Cambodian spiders on sale in a Phnom Penh market.

A further classic urban legend is the 'spider in the hair bun' story.[3] It narrates the cruel fate of a woman whose hairdresser styled her hair into a high bouffant chignon, steadying it with

hair lacquer. A day later the lady felt an acute pain in her head,
but the doctor consulted did not find anything. The pain grew
ever stronger and some days later the woman died. The post-
mortem autopsy revealed that a spider had got into her chignon
but later could not get out because of the lacquer. Being hungry,
the spider then drilled a hole in the skull and sucked out the

cerebrospinal fluid – we find here an interesting connection to the old motif of a spider sitting on the brain. Variations of the story locate the spider in the now popular dreadlocks.

There exist also similar stories which tell us of an exotic journey to southern countries – be it Mexico, South America or India – untertaken by a young woman. She returns home with a mysterious bump on her head, which on closer inspection contains nothing else than a nest of small spiders. This bump splits just in the moment the woman looks at herself in the mirror. The victim is shocked, loses consciousness and according to some accounts even dies. Of course this is an even more fantastic story, without the slightest connections to zoological and physiological reality.

The victims are always females who have journeyed alone to exotic countries, and probably had behaved lasciviously there, thus incurring a measure of 'guilt'. Stories current on American internet sites in 1999 spoke about spider bites suffered by women sitting in restaurant toilets. The old association between females and the spider is here once more visible, albeit in an inverted fashion. But in some stories it was a man who got bitten in an aeroplane toilet and died some days later. The story on the internet referred even to an officially sounding (though of course fictive) medical journal to substantiate the claim that a nest of spiders was discovered subsequently in the airplane's toilet.

Let us end here with 'The Redback on the Toilet Seat', the successful song by country singer Slim Newton. This tongue in cheek story tells the tale of a painful encounter with a male redback spider in a toilet (in reality only female spiders can bite). One line might in some ways serve as a motto for the whole genre of urban spider legends:

I jumped up high in the air and when I hit the ground,
that crafty redback spider wasn't nowhere to be found.

9 Spider Goes Hollywood

Both the spider himself and the persons or organizations that have taken his name played a very important role in the films of the twentieth century.[1] In the last thirty years almost three dozen 'spider films' have been produced, making the spider one of the most popular cinematic animals. Though the great majority of these films are B- or even C-rate films, the popularity of the spider is certainly not a transitory phenomenon, but has deeper roots and reasons.[2]

A start was made in the early days of the history of the cinema by detective and crime films, with the spider or spiders standing for a great criminal or – if used in the plural sense – for larger criminal organizations. The great German film director Fritz Lang presented in 1920 a fantastic two-part silent movie located in the then far-off San Francisco (*The Spiders*, Germany 1919/ 920). A young millionaire and amateur detective battled with a criminal organization intent on taking over the world. The gang – appropriately named 'The Spiders' – had its base in an underground bunker hide-out and was ruled by an iron-fisted femme fatale called 'Supreme Spider'. Unsurprisingly, the adventurous detective managed to defeat the forces of evil single-handed, with the latter portrayed in a way very much prefiguring similar schematic malign groupings depicted later in James

Bond books and films. In this movie the symbolism of the spider already shows close connections to femme fatale imagery, and to intrigues and murders, and is linked with an underground hide-out.

More than twenty years later the Hollywood director Roy William Neill presented in his movie *Sherlock Holmes and the Spider Woman* (1944) a much more sophisticated variant of the

Stills from Sam Raimi's 2002 *Spider-Man* and 2004 *Spider-Man 2*.

'femme fatale as spider' motif. The famous detective got involved in solving the mystery of a whole series of seemingly unrelated suicides. Soon he succeeded in linking them with the activities of a gang led by a woman. The latter lent money to ruined gamblers, forcing them to take out life insurance. Some days later a giant spider entered their bedrooms, his sting resulting in strong hallucinatory effects which caused one gambler after another to commit suicide.

Adroitly faking his own death, Sherlock Holmes ultimately succeeded in demasking the criminal 'spider lady'. Regardless of the convoluted plot, it is the fascinating overlay of three interpretative and semantic levels that must now occupy our attention. The giant spider in the film constitutes a simple and direct reference to spider symbolism; on a more advanced second level we see an evil woman as a spidery and criminal femme fatale. In conversation with his friend Dr Watson in the film, Holmes had said that only a woman could be as refined, careful and ruthless – enumerating thus those psychological attributes of the spider that were to define his reception during the whole twentieth century. On a third and no doubt most sophisticated level we can admire the supreme investigative 'strategy of the spider' pursued by the famous detective, since setting a refined trap – which he did here – is an obvious prerogative of the spider. The concept of a metaphorically meant 'strategy of the spider' was to return in the famous film by Bernardo Bertolucci, *La Strategia del Ragno* (1969), but was applied there to the domain of political intrigue and mythology.

Two films issued in 1986 referred in different ways to the combination of femme fatale and spider topoi. Bob Rafelson's *Black Widow* used the titular reference to the famous spider species prone to kill their mating partners to create a metaphorical reference to a scheming lady intent on killing her successive

rich husbands. However the countermeasures taken by a female FBI agent pretending to be her friend also belong to the domain of a 'spider strategy'. Hector Babenco's more ambitious Brazilian *Kiss of the Spider Woman*, based on the novel by Manuel Puig, placed the story of the spider-woman as a kind of referential movie story set within a wider, encompassing film narration. The titular spider-woman was living on an uninhabited island, and rescued a shipwrecked man, giving him a new lease of life. On the face of it in Rafelson's movie the spider-woman did receive a positive symbolic connotation for the first time ever; her power was still based on the tactics of an entrapment, though this time it was benign.

A second group of spider films can be found in the popular B-movies of the 1950s showing aggressive mutant spiders. A stereotypic leitmotif was provided by an miscarried laboratory experiment resulting in the growth of a monstrous spider, to name only Jack Arnold's *Tarantula* (1955), where a giant tarantula attacks the reckless scientist before being finally annihilated through the use of napalm. In this film the spider comes to represent the dark, the night side of the hero's psyche. Two years later the same director created the film *The Incredible Shrinking*

A poster for Jack
Arnold's 1955 film
Tarantula.

Terror in Arnold's
Tarantula.

Man, in which the titular hero, who had shrunk in a somewhat Kafkaesque way to Lilliputian shape, had then to flee before a dangerous cat. He finally reaches a cellar where he has to fight a life and death- struggle with a much greater spider. As a final gesture before he is about to dwindle to the size of a particle, the shrivelling protagonist arms himself with a pin and slays the spider. The movie represents in a stereotypic way male fears in regard to the vicious female spider. The victorious fight of the shrunken man with the spider in the cellar might however also be interpreted as a symbol of an successful psychotherapy of the deep inner recesses of the masculine soul.

One year later (1958) it was the turn of another B-movie, namely Bert Gordon's *Earth vs. the Spider.* This film directly linked a great spider living in a cellar with the twin issues of sin and morbid sexuality. It portrayed the love of a young couple and showed two attacks perpetrated on a small city by a terrifying spider. The spider appears threateningly in situations displaying

From Jack Arnold's 1957 film *The Incredible Shrinking Man.*

both an overt but also a more subtly experienced eroticism. When the young lovers with their true and decent feelings for each other enter the cave where the spider lives, the dark chamber refers obviously to the dark forces of eros, the spider in turn standing symbolically for evil and the ensuing punishment. A first attempt to kill the spider by using firearms and DDT had to fail, since poison (DDT) cannot really overcome poison (spider) and bullets cannot really hit an amorphous creature. At the very end the spider is however successfully electrocuted, a form of punishment very much congruent with the American punishment ethos of the 1950s. After 1980 some films took up once more the motif of the spider as a pure and simple-minded symbol of evil (for example the Italian film *The Spider's Nest* of 1982).

Whereas the horror science fiction and spider-monster movies of the 1950s reflected fears of an eventual atomic war and of a looming communist invasion, the horror and science-fiction spider-films which appeared in the 1970s echoed a changed world

From Bert Gordon's 1958 film *Earth vs. the Spider*.

in which the feeling of an ecological crisis and an approaching exhaustion of resources was gaining ground. From the very start of the then nascent film genre showing the revolt of mistreated nature, spiders played a prominent role. In the *Kingdom of the Spiders* (John 'Bud' Cardos, 1977) the previously unrestricted use of pesticides resulted in a dramatic increase of spiders which started to attack the inhabitants of a small American town. There follows the usual scheme of initial disbelief, delayed reaction and incoherent first attempts at combating the intruders, to mention only the morally dubious countermeasure of spraying chemical substances against them from the air. These measures could not of course but fail and the film's tarantulas – 5,000 real tarantulas had been imported for the purposes of the movie from Mexico – can be seen successfully taking over the town. These latter scenes are perhaps the most dramatic and spine-chilling images of agitated and aggressive spiders ever shown on film. The last scene shows a picturesque valley with the small city inside, the latter now covered totally by a giant spider's cocoon.

From John Cardos's 1977 film *Kingdom of the Spiders*.

Cardos's film espouses a somewhat heavy handed ecological didacticism, with human guilt for civilizational misdevelopments constituting a moralizing leitmotif and with the spiders empowered to execute the judgement of history and of a mistreated nature. In 1977 the director Stuart Hagmann showed in *Tarantula: The Deadly Cargo* a much more realistic possibility, partly verified by later developments (we have already mentioned the translocation of poisonous Australian spiders to Japan). A coffee sack bursts in a freight plane transporting coffee and illegal migrants; liberated tarantulas subsequently cause the plane to crash. Step by step they take over an adjacent orange plantation and then invade a small city in the vicinity. There ensues a bitter fight between humans and spiders, the arachnoids personifying the vast array of exotic dangers brought home due to the vagaries of commerce, tourism and globalization, though the latter term as such was not in popular use in the 1970s.

In the 1990s this film genre shed its ecological pretences and reverted partly to its horror 'science laboratory' origins. In keeping

From Stuart Hagmann's 1977 film *Tarantulas: The Deadly Cargo.*

with the changed mood of the times the now predominant mutant theme now highlighted actual problems of genetical engineering. The first spider film of the 1990s, Frank Marshall's widely acclaimed *Arachnophobia* (1990) formulated a number of almost classical topoi and solutions which were to appear in a number of other, somewhat less known spider films after that date. In this film a biologist by the name of Dr Atherton searches in Venezuela's tropical forests for unknown spider species. Dr Atherton's photographer has however been stung to deadly effect by an unknown spider, and no antidote against the spider's poison is available. The corpse of the photographer has been flown back to America and the murderous spider has managed to hide himself in the coffin, sucking all the blood out of the body during the journey – the following view of the completely mumified corpse is one of the strongest anti-arachnoid shockers of the film. Soon afterwards in an adjacent small city people begin to die from unknown causes. A newly arrived physician, Dr Jennings, who since his infancy has suffered from a severe

From Frank Marshall's 1990 film *Arachnophobia*.

form of arachnophobia, links the deaths to the fact that all of the victims have been previously stung by a spider.

He is able to establish the fact that a genetic mutation has occured and that the alien spider (a commanding spider in the fashion of ants and bees) has copulated successfully with domestic spiders, creating a new dangerous species. The final scenes of the film are designed to evoke feelings of horror in a person with arachnophobic tendencies: Dr Atherton discovers the commanding spiders's lair in the house of Dr Jennings and is killed subsequently by a multitude of arachnoids leaving Dr Jennings with the unenviable task of facing them alone. Jennings protects his family, who have been surrounded and threatened by hundreds of spiders and then – overcoming his own arachnophobia – wins the final battle with the commanding spider, this typical filmic final showdown taking place once more in a cellar heavily endowed with symbolic references. The ugly and grim-looking Avondale (*Delena cancerides)* New Zealand spiders succeeded in evoking feelings of fear and revulsion among the spectators – in reality however these creatures are totally harmless.

Two films from the beginning of the twenty-first century, namely *Spiders* (Gary Jones, 2000) and *Spiders 2* (Sam Firstenberg, 2001) once more refer to scientific experiments, the first movie conducting them in a space exploration laboratory. In the film directed by Jones a DNA-vaccination morphs a tarantula to gigantic proportions. It first attacks the crew of a spaceship and then the inhabitants of a small city. The movie uses references to the topoi of the 'Great Mother' in a rather ironic way, since the murderous King-Kong-size tarantula goes under the name of 'Mother-in-law'.

The second movie provides a variation of some motifs of the first. Let us mention also two 'catastrophic' spider movies (*The Giant Spider Invasion,* Bill Rebane, 1975) and *Creepies* (Jeff Leroy, 2003), which deploy – despite the lapse between them of almost thirty years – very similar thematic clichés in a fairly straightforward mode and on a very primitive staging level. In

From Jeff Leroy's
2003 film *Creepies.*

A film still from
Sam Raimi's 2007
Spider-Man 3.

the more recent film giant 'killer spiders' which escaped from a
military laboratory start a lightning attack on Hollywood and
have to be beaten back by a regular army operation using rockets
and combat helicopters. After two days, almost a half of the Cali-
fornian film metropolis was in ruins.

We have to end our narrative with Sam Raimi's popular *Spider-
Man* films (2002, 2004, 2007) in which the hero – seen mostly
in a positive light – combats the world of vice and crime with
the help of 'spidery' physical abilities acquired through a spider
sting. The spider in question had been genetically modified,
hence the particular efficacy of his sting. Raimi shows however
that some spider traits, like gyrating in the net, do not come
easily to our hero, since the world of humans and the world of
spiders do differ.

The spider films show, as already indicated, a number of common characteristics: fear of the spiderous femme fatale, spider
poison in the service of mutations and transmogrifications
but also sometimes serving as an straightforward killing instrument, spiders as criminals, dark cellars as the spider's lair and
so on. However the staging of spider attacks is less picturesque

than the doings of King Kong, hence the recent career of *Spider-Man*. And on the whole, film spiders prefer to invade and take over small cities, only rarely targeting metropolitan agglomerations. One reason for this could be the fact that small cities could revert more easily to their natural pre-urban shape.

On a deeper level the filmic attack of the spiders symbolize the dissolution of form and bodily cohesion. Bodies become dissolved, dried out or conversely liquefied; they lose their shape in manifold ways; a small city becomes totally entangled by the web and is thus deprived of its silhouette. The web or cocoon might even fulfil these functions without the existence of its creator, the spider: in the once celebrated movie *The Invasion of the Body Snatchers* (Philip Kaufmann, 1978) the aliens as enemies of the human race start their terrestrial invasion in form of a gigantic spider's web, a web which kills human beings and subsequently converts their bodies into an amorphous mass.

Lovis Corinth's 1894 etching *The End.*

In early May 2009 a great number of press releases and internet notices described a reported invasion of the small Australian town of Bowen by eastern tarantulas.[3] When the early excitement subsided after a week or so it became – in view of the small number of spiders involved – quite clear that the much over-dramatized invasion amounted to nothing more than an attempt at a reenactment of a Hollywood spider movie plot: the wheel had indeed come full circle.

SPIDERS AND MODERN CIVILIZATION

In this book we have tried to illustrate and analyse the astounding career of the spider in the twentieth century. Let us, in lieu of conclusion, point to one more important point. To put it somewhat simplistically, modern civilization is characterized by a continuing obfuscation of the relations between subject and object. What is more, both political and sociological processes, and the worlds of microelectronics and that of a computer generated 'virtual reality' are being characterized more and more by a sort of vacuity at the centre.

Seen from that perspective the spider seems to conform by his outward appearance and his actions with these civilizational trends. Like Macavity the mystery cat he is both at the centre of his web and not there; we fear him and fear him not; and we suffer, as arachnophobes, from millions of almost wholly imaginary spider bites. The physical reality of the spider can be swept away by a mere gust of wind, the web is both seemingly immaterial and a very real tough barrier; tangibility and vacuity thus vie for primacy. Are we indulging in rhetorical hyperbole by suggesting that the spider has become now one of the emblematic creatures of the post-industrial world? It is for the reader to decide.

Timeline of the Spider

140 million years BC	9000–8500 BC	6th century BC	8 AD
Earliest extant spider web encased in amber	Earliest pictogram of a spider, found near Göbekli Tepe (Anatolia)	Heraclitus of Ephesus compares the sensory faculties of man and the spider	Ovid tells the story of the weaver Arachne's transmogrification into a spider

1678	1690–1710	1890–94
Martin Lister publishes the first book on spiders in England	The German botanical and zoological artist Maria Sibylla Merian depicts spider species in a particularly naturalist mode	Henry McCook publishes his fundamental *American Spiders and their Spinning Work*

1922	1950s	1990s
Freud's follower Karl Abraham publishes his classic psychoanalytic spider study *The Spider as a Dream Symbol*	The first Hollywood horror films about mutant spiders appear	The World Wide Web is compared to the spider's web

AD 100–800	4th century AD	1236–1250	1624
The Moche culture in Peru uses the image of the spider	Basil the Great compares heretics to spiders	Thomas of Cantimpré associates spiders with the sense of touch (*tactus*)	Francis Bacon compares theoretical scientists ('reasoners') to spiders constructing a web

c. 1900	1907	1920
Spiders appear often as an Art Nouveau pictorial motif	The German writer Hanns Heinz Evers creates the classic spider horror story in his short story 'The Spider'	The famous German film director Fritz Lang creates the first spider film referring to criminal deeds in his *The Spiders*

1994–5	2008	2009
Beginnings of the spider motif by Louise Bourgeois	*La Princesse*, a giant mechanical spider, starts her triumphal march in Liverpool	The earliest extant spider web encased in amber found in Hastings, Sussex

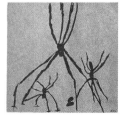

References

INTRODUCTION: SPIDERS ON THE WALL AND ELSEWHERE

1 Martin Brasier, Laura Cotton and Ian Yenny, 'First Report of Amber with Spider Webs and Microbial Inclusions from the Early Cretaceous (*c.* 140 Ma) of Hastings, Sussex', *Journal of the Geological Society*, 166 (December 2009), pp. 989–97.
2 Nancy Mitford, *Böse Gedanken einer englischen Lady* (Reinbek, 1996), p. 32.
3 Tim Berners-Lee, BCS *Lovelace Lecture*, London, 13 March 2007.

1 SOME BASIC ZOOLOGICAL FACTS

1 The shelf of spider books is a very long one. We mention here only those that we have found especially stimulating or useful: John Crompton, *Life of the Spider* (London, 1955); Dick Jones, *The Country Life Guide to Spiders of Britain and Northern Europe* (London, 1983); Stefan Heimer and Wolfgang Nentwig, *Spinnen Mitteleuropas* (Berlin, 1991); Paul Hillyard, *The Book of the Spider: From Arachnophobia to the Love of Spiders* (London, 1994); Ken Preston-Mafham and Rod Preston-Mafham, *The Natural History of Spiders* (Ramsbury, 1996); Adrienne Mason, *The World of the Spider* (San Francisco, CA, 1999).
2 *Guardian*, 19 June 2001. When writing the book we believed this information, but it has now been revealed as an urban legend. See the internet platform *The Spider Myths Site* run by

the Burke Museum of Natural History, Seattle (www.washington. edu/burkemuseum/spider_myth) commentary by Rod Crawford, 14 October 2008,

3 Interview with their discoverer, Ingo Rechenberg, 'Rollende Spinnen für den Mars', *Frankfurter Allgemeine Zeitung*, 10 January 2009.

4 A wonderful photo of a 'gift introduction' in Mason, *The World of the Spider*, p. 48.

5 Christopher J. Meehan, Eric J. Olson, Matthew W. Reudink, T. Kurt Kyser and Robert L. Curry, 'Herbivory in Spider Through Exploitation of an Ant-plant Mutualism', *Current Biology*, xix/19, 13 October 2009. It is symptomatic of public interest in spiders that these findings were announced in the mainstream press on the very day of the article's issue by the *Daily Telegraph*: Tom Chivers, 'Vegetarian Spider Bagheera Kiplingi found in Central America', 13 October 2009.

6 Erwin Tretzel, 'Die Sprache bei Spinnen', *Umschau*, LXIII (1963), pp. 372–6.

7 Diemut Klärner, 'Rätselhafte Spinnenseide. Röntgenstrahlen beleuchten die molekularen Details', *Frankfurter Allgemeine Zeitung*, 4 May 2007.

8 Günther Stockinger, 'Brücke für neue Nerven', *Der Spiegel*, 50 (2008), p. 168.

2 ARACHNOPHOBIA

1 The literature about arachnophobia is somewhat patchy, no synthetic study having been attempted until now. See however T. H. Savory, *Spiders, Men and Scorpions* (London, 1961); H. Beerman and W. B. Nutting, 'Arachnid-Related Phobias: Symbiophobia, Prevention and Treatment', in *Mammalian Diseases and Arachnids*, II, ed. W. B. Nutting (Roca Baton, 1984), pp. 103–12; T. N. Hardy, 'Entomophobia: The Case for Miss Muffet', *Bulletin of the Entomological Society of America*, XXXIV (1988), pp. 64–9; Primo Levi, *Other People's Trades* (London, 1989),

pp. 141–5; Franz Renner, *Spinnen ungeheuer-sympathisch* (Kaiserslautern,1990), pp. 59–85; G.C.L. Davey, 'Characteristics of Individuals with Fear of Spiders', *Anxiety Research*, IV (1992), pp. 299–314; G.C.L. Davey, 'The "Disgusting" Spider: The Role of Disease and Illness in the Perpetuation of Fear of Spiders', *Society and Animals: Journal of Human-Animal Studies*, II (1994); Paul Hillyard, *The Book of the Spider: From Arachnophobia to the Love of Spiders* (London, 1994), pp. 3–15; M. K. Jones, S. Whitmont and R. G. Menzies, 'Danger Expectancies and Insight in Spider Phobia', *Anxiety*, II/4 (1996), pp. 179–85; Antje B.M. Gerdes, Gabriele Uhl and Georg W. Alpers, 'Spiders are Special: Fear and Disgust Evoked by Pictures of Arthropods', *Evolution and Human Behaviour: Official Journal of the Human Behaviour and Evolution Society* (online), XXX (January 2009), pp. 66–73.

2 See Hillyard, *The Book of the Spider*, p. 6; R. R. Cornelius and J. R. Averil, 'Sex Differences in Fear of Spiders', *Journal of Personality and Social Psychology*, XLV (1983), pp. 377–83.

3 On tarantism see *inter alia* H. F. Gloyne, 'Tarantism: Mass Hysterical Reaction to Spider Bite in the Middle Ages', *American Image*, VII (1950), pp. 29–42; J. F. Russell, 'Tarantism', *Medical History*, XXIII (1979), pp. 404–25.

3 VENOM AND COLD INTELLECT: THE SPIDER AND ITS WEB
IN THE EUROPEAN INTELLECTUAL TRADITION

1 'Spider', in *The Jewish Encyclopedia* (New York and London, 1904), vol. VI, p. 607.

2 John Manning, *The Emblem* (London, 2004), p. 108.

3 Sherwood Owen Dickinson, 'Ancient Illustrations of Animal Intelligence', *Transactions and Proceedings of the American Philological Associations*, XLII (1911), pp. 124–5.

4 Nicander, *The Poems and Poetical Fragments* (London and Cambridge, MA, 1953), p. 29.

5 Claudian, *Rape of Proserpine III* (London and Cambridge, MA, 1956), vol. III, p. 357.

6 Seneca, *Ad Lucillium Epistulae Morales* (London and Cambridge, MA, 1953), vol. III, pp. 408–12.

7 M. L. Welles, *Arachne's Tapestry: The Transformation of Myth in Seventeenth-Century Spain* (San Antonio, TX, 1986). The last contribution is by Karin Hellwig, 'Aby Warburg und das "Weberinnenbild" von Diego Velázquez', *Zeitschrift für Kunstgeschichte*, LXIX (2006), pp. 548–60.

8 Hermann Diels, *Die Fragmente der Vorsokratiker* (Berlin, 1951), vol. I, p. 166.

9 Walter Böhm, *Johannes Philoponus Grammatikos von Alexandrien* (Munich, 1967), p. 208.

10 Ambrose, *Ennarationes in Psalmos,* XXXVIII, in J. P. Migne, *Patrologia Latina*, vol. XIV, p. 1106.

11 *Thesaurus Proverbiorum Medii Aevi* (Berlin and New York, 2001), vol. XI, p. 67.

12 Cassiodorus, *Expositio in Psalterium*, in Migne, *Patrologia Latina*, vol. LXX, pp. 284–5.

13 St Thomas Aquinatis, *In octo Libros Physicorum Aristoteli Expositia*, ed. P. M. Maggiolo (Rome, 1965), p. 127.

14 Louise Vinge, *The Five Senses: Studies in a Literary Tradition* (Lund, 1975), pp. 50–51.

15 Carl Nordenfalk, 'The Five Senses in Flemish Art before 1600', in Görel Cavalli-Björkman, *Netherlandish Mannerism* (Stockholm, 1985), pp. 135–54.

16 Shakespeare, *Midsummer Night's Dream,* Act II, Scene ii; *King Richard II,* Act III, Scene ii; *The Winter's Tale,* Act II, Scene i.

17 Leonardo da Vinci, *Fabeln* (Leipzig, 1978), pp. 9, 20, 88.

18 Barbara Haeger, 'Rubens' *Adoration of the Magi* and the Program for the High Altar of St Michael's Abbey in Antwerp', *Simiolus,* XXV (1997), p. 60.

19 John Bunyan, *A Book for Boys and Girls: or Country Rhymes for Children* (facsimile London, 1889), XVII, pp. 18–25. see also Rosemary Freeman, *English Emblem Books* (New York, 1966), pp. 209–18.

20 J. W. Cunliffe, ed., *The Works of George Gascoigne* (Cambridge,

1907), p. 476. See also Sergiusz Michalski, 'Der Biene-Spinne Vergleich in der theologischen Polemik des konfessionellen Zeitalters', in *Art, réligion et sociètè dans l'espace germanique au XVI siècle*, ed. Frank Muller (Strasbourg, 1997), pp. 117–32.

21 *The Works of Francis Bacon* (Stuttgart, 1963), vol. IV – *Novum Organum*, pp. 92f.

22 Judith Dundas, *The Spider and the Bee: The Artistry of Spenser's Faerie Queene* (Urbana and Chicago, 1985).

23 Jonathan Swift, *The Battle of the Books* (Berlin and New York, 1978), pp. 8–11. See Herman-Josef Real, 'Die Biene und die Spinne in Swifts *Battle of the Books*', *Germanisch-Romanische Monatsschrift*, XXIII (1973), pp. 169–77.

24 Edward Young, *Night Thoughts* VI, 208–12, in *The Complete Works* (London, 1854), vol. I, p. 99.

25 Ted Morgan, *Somerset Maugham* (London, 1981), p. 105.

26 Karl Möseneder, *Franz Anton Maulbertsch. Aufklärung in der barocken Deckenmalerei* (Vienna-Cologne-Weimar, 1993), p. 126.

27 'Araignée', *Encyclopédie ou dictionnaire raisonné* (Paris, 1751), vol. I, pp. 572–4.

28 Leon Schwartz, 'L'image de l'araignée dans *Le Rêve de D'Alembert* de Diderot', *Romance Notes*, XV (1973/4), pp. 264–7.

29 Denis Diderot, *Oeuvres philosophiques* (Paris, 1961) pp. 314–15.

30 Georges Poulet, *The Metamorphoses of the Circle* (Baltimore, MD, 1966), p. 55

31 Montesquieu, *Essai sur les causes qui peuvent affecter les esprits et les caractères. Oeuvres complètes* (Paris, 1951), vol. II, p. 49.

32 Alexander Pope, *Essay on Man*, Epistle I.

33 Tommaso Gaudiosi, *La Ragna*, in *Marino e i Marinisti*, ed. Giuseppe Guido Ferrero (Milan, 1954), p. 1080.

34 Berthold Brockes, *Irdisches Vergnügen in Gott* [1738] (Berne, 1970), pp. 247–53.

35 Leland I. Warren, 'Poetic Vision and the Natural World: The Spider and his Web in the Poetry of William Blake', *Enlightenment Essays*, VI (1975), pp. 50–62.

36 Michelangelo Buonarroti, *Rime* (Milan, 1954), LXXXI, p. 76. See

also Horst Bredekamp, 'Grillenfänge von Michelangelo bis Goethe', *Marburger Jahrbuch für Kunstwissenschaft*, XXII (1989), p. 173.

37 This translation is by Erich Auerbach, *Scenes from the Drama of European Literature* (Gloucester, MA, 1973), p. 202.

38 Victor Hugo, *Oeuvres poètiques* (Paris, 1967), vol. II, p. 785.

39 Victor Hugo, *La Légende des siècles* [1856] (Paris, 1974), strophe VIII.

40 Victor Hugo, *Notre-Dame de Paris. 1482. Les Travailleurs de la mer* (Bourges, 1975), p. 278.

4 THE FEMME FATALE AND EROTICISM

1 Hanns Heinz Ewers, *Die Spinne*, in Hanns Heinz Ewers, *Die Besessenen. Seltsame Geschichten* (Munich, 1908), pp. 101–46.

2 Theophrastus Paracelsus, *Liber Principiorum* (1527) repr. in Theophrastus Paracelsus, *Bücher und Schriften* (Hildesheim, 1972), ed. J. Huser, vol. III, p. 286.

3 Xenophon, *Memorabilia*, I, 3, 11-14.

4 Pieter J. J. van Thiel, 'Willem Buytewech's Dignified Couples Courting: A Rule of Conduct for Young Noblemen Entangled in Venus's Trap', *Simiolus*, XXXII (2006), pp. 35–58, here pp. 39–40.

5 Ibid., text on ill.15, p. 52.

6 Christian-Heinrich Spieß, *Biographien der Wahnsinnigen* (Neuwied-Berlin, 1969), p. 311.

7 Jeremias Gotthelf, *Die schwarze Spinne* [1842], ed. Klaus Lindemann (Paderborn, 1982).

8 Ronald D. LeBlanc, 'Trapped in a Spider's Web of Animal Lust: Human Bestiality in Lev Gumilevsky's *Dog Alley*', *The Russian Review*, LXV (2006), pp. 171–93, esp. pp. 180–83.

9 Peter Dettmanig, 'Die Spinnen-Metapher in Dostojewskis *Dämonen*', in *Kunstbefragung. Dreißig Jahre psychoanalytische Werkinterpretation*, ed. Gisela Greve (Tübingen, 1996).

10 Aleksandr Zakrzhevskii, *Kharamazovshchina: Psikhologicheskie paralleli* (Kiev, 1912), p. 149.

11 LeBlanc, 'Trapped in a Spider's Web of Animal Lust', pp. 176–81.

12 Frank Daniel, *Die Frau bei Baudelaire* (Erlangen and Nuremberg, 1965), pp. 78–9.

13 Remy de Gourmont, *The Natural Philosophy of Love* (1903), trans. Ezra Pound (New York, 1931), p. 84.

14 Lester Ward, *Pure Sociology* (1903) quoted after Bram Dijkstra, *Evil Sisters: The Threat of Female Sexuality and the Cult of Manhood* (New York, 1996), p. 68.

15 Williamson's story was published in the pulp magazine *Weird Tales* (1932). We follow here the analysis and the quotations in Dijkstra, *Evil Sisters*, pp. 142–5.

16 Dijkstra, *Evil Sisters*, p. 145.

17 Theresa Ann Gronberg, 'Femme de Brasserie', *Art History*, VII (September 1984), p. 333.

18 Katharina A. Lochnan, *Seductive Surfaces: The Art of Tissot* (New Haven and London, 1999), p. 37.

19 The last, not always pertinent analysis in Andrew Wilton, ed., *Der Symbolismus in England 1860–1910*, exh. cat. (Ostfildern-Ruit, 1998), p. 224 (by Simon Wilson).

20 Christoph Brockhaus, *Alfred Kubin. Das zeichnerische Frühwerk bis 1904*, exh. cat. (Kunsthalle Baden-Baden, 1977), pp. 150–51.

21 A. A. Sidorov, *Russkaja grafika nachala xx vieka* (Moscow, 1969), pp. 154–5.

22 *Die Jugend* (1903) no. 51, p. 537.

5 OPPRESSIVE MOTHERS, DREAMS AND LOUISE BOURGEOIS

1 Published in German in 1922. English translation in *The International Journal of Psycho-Analysis*, IV (1923), pp. 313–17. (Often reprinted, starting with Karl Abraham, *The Selected Papers of Karl Abraham* (London, 1927), pp. 326–32).

2 Ibid., p. 315.

3 Ibid., p. 317.

4 Sigmund Freund, *Gesammelte Werke* (London, 1940), vol. xv, p. 25.

5 Ralph B. Little, 'Spider Phobias', *Psychoanalytical Quarterly*, XXXVI

(1967), pp. 51–60.

6 Ralph B. Little, 'Umbilical Cord Symbolism of the Spider's Dropline' *Psychoanalytical Quarterly*, XXXV (1966), pp. 587–90.

7 Carl Gustav Jung, 'Ein moderner Mythus' (1958), in *Gesammelte Werke* (Olten-Freiburg im Breisgau, 1978), vol. X, p. 383.

8 Ibid., pp. 385–6.

9 Carl Gustav Jung, 'Der philosophische Baum' [1954] in *Gesammelte Werke*, vol. XIII, p. 363.

10 Alberto Giacometti, 'Le rêve, le sphinx et la mort de T', published in *Labyrinthe*, no. 22/23 (December 1946), pp. 12–13, reprinted in Alberto Giacometti, *Ecrits* (Paris, 1990), pp. 27–37. See also Christine Bouche, *Alberto Giacometti, La femme, le sphinx, l'effroi* (Paris, 2004).

11 J. A. Hadfield, *Dreams and Nightmares* (Harmondsworth, 1969), pp. 193–4.

12 Friedrich Seifert and Rotraut Seifert-Helwig, *Bilder und Urbilder. Erscheinungsformen des Archetypus* (Munich and Basle, 1965), pp. 122–3, 209.

13 Maria Elisabeth Wollschläger and Gerhard Wollschläger, *Der Schwan und die Spinne. Das konkrete Symbol in Diagnostie und Psychotherapie* (Berne, 1998), p. 104.

14 Ingrid Sischy, interview with Louise Bourgeois, www.procuniarworkshop.com, Interview 1997 (accessed 8 October 2006). See also Mieke Bal, 'Narrative Inside Out: Louise Bourgeois' Spider as Theoretical Object', *Oxford Art Journal*, XXII/2 (1999), pp. 101–26.

6 SPIDERS IN ART AND CARICATURE

1 See an instructive comparison of two images of the transformed Arachne from 1473 and 1641 in Betty Kurth, 'Arachne', in *Reallexikon zur Deutschen Kunstgeschichte*, vol. I, (Stuttgart, 1937), pp. 900–1.

2 See Ulrike Spyra, *Das "Buch der Natur" des Konrad von Megenberg* (Cologne, 1975), ill. 96.

3 Joris Hoefnagel, *Archetypa Studiaque Patris Georgii Hoefnagelii. Nature, Poetry and Science in Art around 1600*, exh. cat., ed. Th.Vignau-Wilberg (Munich, 1994), plates on pages 99, 107, 109, 143.

4 Samuel van Hoogstraten, *Inleiding tot de hooge schoole der schilderkonst* (Rotterdam, 1678), p. 123.

5 Ingvar Bergström, 'Disguised Symbolism in *'Madonna'* Pictures in Still-Lifes: II', *Burlington Magazine*, XCIII/633 (September 1955), p. 346.

6 Especially fine watercolour depictions of spiders made by Maria Sibylla Merian are kept in the Archives of the Academy of Arts, St Petersburg.

7 See for example Grandville, *The Spider and the Lark*, in *Das gesamte Werk* (Munich, 1969), vol. I, p. 559.

8 Vanessa Sigalas, 'Animalische Symbole und Äquivalenzen der Frau im Glas des Jugendstils', MA thesis, University of Tübingen, Institute of Art History (2006), pp. 68–73.

9 For example *The Studio*, XXXII (1904), p. 365; vol. XXXIV (1905), pp. 151, 193; vol. XXXVII (1906), p. 89.

10 Morris Rosenfeld, *Lieder des Ghetto*, trans. Berthold Feivel (Berlin, 1903) – many subsequent editions.

11 Donald W. Druick, ed., *Redon 1840–1916*, exh. cat., Art Institute of Chicago et al. (1994/5), pp. 149–53.

12 Jules Michelet, *L'insecte* (Paris, 1858), pp. 210, 219, 223.

13 Druick, *Redon 1840–1916*, note 35, p. 400.

14 See esp. Jürgen Döring,'Der Mensch-Tier Vergleich: die Spinne als Zeichen', in *Mittel und Motive der Karikatur in fünf Jahrhunderten. Bild als Waffe*, ed. Gerhard Langemeyer (Munich, 1984), S. 238–49.

15 Wolfgang Harms and Beate Rattay, *Illustrierte Flugblätter aus den Jahrhunderten der Reformation und der Glaubenskämpfe* (Coburg, 1983), cat. no. 78.

16 Otto Baur, *Bestiarium Humanum. Mensch-Tier-Vergleich in Kunst und Karikatur.* (Gräfelfing, 1974), p. 136.

17 We used the German edition: Gustave Doré, *Die äusserst anschau-*

liche, fesselnde und seltsame Historie vom Heiligen Russland
(Gütersloh, 1970), p. 183.

18 For anti-Semitic postcards characterizing Jews as spiders, see
Herbert Gold, Georg Heuberger, ed., *Abgestempelt. Judenfeindliche
Postkarten.* exh. cat. Postmuseum und Jüdisches Museum
(Frankfurt am Main, 1999), pp. 313, 316–17, 325.

19 Ralph E. Shikes, *The Indignant Eye: The Artist as Social Critic in
Prints and Drawings from the Fifteenth Century to Picasso* (Boston,
1969), pp. 374–6.

20 For Kubin's spider images and the out-of-scale series by other
draughtsmen see Christoph Brockhaus, *Alfred Kubin. Das zeichnerische Frühwerk bis 1904,* exh. cat. (Kunsthalle Baden-Baden, 1977),
pp. 60–61, 202, 222–5.

21 Christian Klemm, ed., *Alberto Giacometti*, exh. cat. (Kunsthaus
Zurich, 2001), p. 140.

22 See Claudia Spiess, *Germaine Richier (1902-1959), Die lebendig
gewordene Skulptur.* (Hildesheim, 1998), p. 120, however without
reference to Giacometti.

23 Klaus Schmidt, *Sie bauten die ersten Tempel. Das rätselhafte
Heiligtum der Steinzeitjäger* (Munich, 2006).

24 Ernst Scheyer, 'Der Symbolgehalt der Ornamentik in der prähi-
storischen Kunst Nord-Amerikas', *Symbolon,* III (1962), pp. 142–85.

7 MYTH AND FOLKLORE

1 The best survey is the book by Bernd Rieken, *Arachne und ihre
Schwestern. Eine Motivgeschichte der Spinne von den
'Naturvölkermärchen' bis zu den 'Urban Legends'* (Münster, 2003).
See also Richard Riegler, 'Spinnenmythus und Spinnenaberglaube
in der neueren Erzählungsliteratur', *Schweizerisches Archiv für
Volkskunde*, XXVI (1926), pp. 55–69, 123–42; Richard Riegler, s. v.
'Spinne', in *Handwörterbuch des Deutschen Aberglaubens,* vol. VIII
(Berlin and Leipzig, 1937), pp. 265–84; W. S. Brisbane, 'Spider
Superstitions and Folklore', *Transactions of the Connecticut
Academy of Arts and Sciences,* XLVI (1945), pp. 53–91; Martha

Weigle, *Spiders and Spinsters: Women and Mythology* (Albuquerque, NM, 1982).

2 See Richard Riegler, 'Spinnenmythus und Spinnenaberglaube in der neueren Erzählungsliteratur', *Schweizerisches Archiv für Volkskunde*, XXVI (1926), pp. 55–69, 123–44; Deborah Chocolate and Dave Albers, *Anansi and the Spider God: An Akan Legend* (New York, 1997); P. M. Sherlock, *Anansi the Spider Man* (London, 1956).

3 Martha Warren Beckwith, *Jamaica Anansi Stories* (New York, 1924)

4 On other African spider stories see Carl Spiess 'Fabeln über die Spinne bei den Ewe am Unterlauf des Volta in Westafrika', *Mitteilungen des Seminars für Orientalische Sprachen zu Berlin. Afrikanische Studien*, XXI–XXII (1918–1919), pp. 101–34; Maurice Delafosse' 'Le Roman de l'Araignée chez les Baoulé de la Cote d'Ivoire', *Revue d'Ethnographie et des Traditions Populaires*, 1/3 (1920), pp. 197–218.

5 Arthur Grimble and Rosemary Grimble, *Migrations, Myth and Magic from the Gilbert Islands* (London, 2004).

6 Karl Taube, 'The Teotihacán Spider Woman', *Journal of Latin American Lore*, IX (1983), pp. 107–89.

7 D. van Hinloopen Labberton 'Über die Bedeutung der Spinne in der indischen Literatur', *Zeitschrift der Deutschen Morgenländischen Gesellschaft*, 66 (1912) pp.605

8 URBAN LEGENDS

1 Rolf-Wilhelm Brednich, *Die Spinne in der Yucca-Palme. Sagenhafte Geschichten von heute* (Munich, 1992). See also Bernd Rieken, *Arachne und ihre Schwestern. Eine Motivgeschichte der Spinne von den 'Naturvölkermärchen' bis zu den 'Urban Legends'* (Münster, 2003), pp. 187–92. There are countless spider urban legends on the internet.

2 Rieken, *Arachne und ihre Schwestern*, pp. 190–91.

3 David Hall and Bill Mooney, *Spiders in the Hairdo: Modern Urban Legends* (Atlanta, GA, 1999), pp. 70–71.

1 Spider films are discussed mostly on the internet, s. v. 'Spider Films' etc., as part of the portal Tierhorror.de (in German).

2 Patric Lucanio, *Them or Us: Archetypal Interpretations of Fifties Alien Invasion Films* (Bloomington, IN, 1987); Bernd Rieken, *Arachne und ihre Schwestern. Eine Motivgeschichte der Spinne von den 'Naturvölkermärchen' bis zu den 'Urban Legends'* (Münster, 2003), pp. 223–43; Thomas Ballhausen,'Horror auf acht Beinen. Eine Notiz zu Spinnen im Film', in Thomas Ballhausen, *Delirium und Extase. Die Aktualität des Monströsen* (Vienna, 2008), pp. 80–83.

3 See the credulous report in *The Times,* 6 May 2009 ('Giant Spiders Invade Australian Outback Town') and the scathing critique by Christine Kellett in the Australian newspaper *Independent Weekly,* 8 May 2009 ('Web of Lies: UK Press Plays Up Spider Invasion').

Select Bibliography

Abraham, Karl, 'The Spider as a Dream Symbol', *The International Journal of Psychoanalysis*, IV (1923), pp. 313–17

Ballhausen, Thomas, *Delirium und Extase. Zur Aktualität des Monströsen* (Vienna, 2008)

Barth, F. G., *Sinne und Verhalten – aus dem Leben einer Spinne* (Heidelberg, 2001)

Brednich, Rolf-Wilhelm, *Die Spinne in der Yucca-Palme. Sagenhafte Geschichten von heute* (Munich, 1992)

Brisbane, W. S., 'Spider Superstitions and Folklore', *Transactions of the Connecticut Academy of Arts and Sciences*, XLVI (1945), pp. 53–91

Bristowe, W. S., *The World of Spiders* (London, 1971)

Chocolate, Deborah, and Dave Albers, *Anansi and the Spider God* (New York, 1997)

Cloudesley-Thompson, J. L., 'Scorpions and Spiders in Mythology and Folklore', in *Scorpions: In Memoriam Gary A. Polis*, ed. V. Fet and P. A. Selden (Burnham Beeches, 2001)

Crompton, John, *Life of the Spider* (London, 1955)

Dittrich, Sigrid, and Lothar Dittrich, 'Spinne', in *Lexikon der Tiersymbolik* (Petersberg, 2004)

Döering, Jürgen, 'Der Mensch-Tier Vergleich. Die Spinne als Zeichen', in *Mittel und Motive der Karikatur aus fünf Jahrhunderten. Bild als Waffe*, ed. Gerhard Langemeyer (Munich, 1984), pp. 238–49

Dundas, Judith, *The Spider and the Bee: The Artistry of Spenser's Faerie Queene* (Urbana, IL, 1985)

Eckardt, Holger, 'Plage des Bösen oder Kleinod des Schöpfers: Von Netz zu Spinne zwischen dem Meissner und Trakl', *Neophilologus*, LXXXI/1 (1997), pp. 105–15

Foelix, R. F., *Biology of Spiders* (Harvard, MA, 1982)

Hall, David, and Bill Mooney, *Spiders in the Hairdo: Modern Urban Legends* (Atlanta, 1999)

Harley, B., and J. Parker, *Martin Lister's English Spiders* (Colchester, 1992)

Heimer, Stefan, and Wolfgang Nentwig, *Spinnen Mitteleuropas* (Berlin, 1991)

Hillyard, Paul, *The Book of the Spider: From Arachnophobia to the Love of the Spiders* (London, 1994)

Jones, Dick, *The Country Life Guide to Spiders of Britain and Northern Europe* (London, 1983)

Journal of Arachnology, vol. I–XXXVII (1973–2009)

Kulessa, Hanna, *Die Spinne. Schaurige und schöne Geschichten* (Frankfurt am Main, 1991)

Lindemann, Klaus, and Raimar Stefan Zons, *Lauter Schwarze Spinnen. Spinnenmotive in der deutschen Literatur. Eine Sammlung* (Bonn, 1990)

Mason, Adrienne, *The World of the Spider* (San Francisco, CA, 1999)

Preston-Mafham, Ken, and Rod Preston-Mafham, *The Natural History of Spiders* (Ramsbury, 1996)

Renner, Franz, *Spinnen, ungeheuer-sympathisch* (Kaiserslautern, 1990)

Riegler, Richard, 'Spinnenmythus und Spinnenaberglaube in der neueren Erzählungsliteratur', *Schweizerisches Archiv für Volkskunde*, XXVI (1926), pp. 55–69, 123–44

—, 'Spinne', in *Handwörterbuch des Deutschen Aberglaubens*, vol. VIII (Leipzig and Berlin, 1937), pp. 265–84

Rieken, Bernd, *Arachne und ihre Schwestern. Eine Motivgeschichte der Spinne von den 'Naturvölkermärchen' bis zu den 'Urban Legends'* (Munster, 2003)

—, 'Die Spinne als Symbol in Volksdichtung und Literatur', *Fabula. Zeitschrift für Erzählforschung*, XXXVI (1995), pp. 187–204

Savory, T. H., *Spiders, Men and Scorpions* (London, 1961)

Shear, W. A., ed., *Spiders, Webs: Behaviour and Evolution* (Stanford, CA, 1986)

Sherlock, P. M., *Anansi the Spider Man* (London, 1956)

Siganos, André, *Les mythologies de l'insecte. Histoire d'une fascination* (Paris, 1985)

Weigle, Martha, *Spiders and Spinsters: Women and Mythology* (Albuquerque, NM, 1982)

Associations and Websites

International Society of Arachnology (ISA) organizes a congress every three years
www.arachnology.org

The European Society of Arachnology (ESA) chooses the European Spider of the Year annually
www.european-arachnology.org

American Arachnological Society (AAS)
www.americanarachnology.org

Australasian Arachnological Society (AAS)
www.australasian-arachnology.org

British Arachnological Society (BAS)
www.british-spiders.org.uk

GENERAL

The Spider Myths Site
www.washington.edu/burkemuseum/Spidermyths/links

Tiere in Horrorfilm (Animals in Horrorfilms)
www.tierhorror.de

Since the internet is bewilderingly replete with spider literature and sites – often quite freakish ones – we have decided to eschew most of the detailed references for phenomena adequately described there.

Acknowledgements

When working on this book we were helped in various ways by Horst Bredekamp, Lorenz Enderlein, Izabella Galicka, Peter Gyllan, Wolfgang Harms, Peter K. Klein, Verena Krieger, Annegret Jürgens-Kirchhoff, Monika Müller, Thomas Raff, Vanessa Sigalas, Reinhard A. Steiner, Anna-Maria Coderch Stoichita and Victor Ieronim Stoichita and Ryszard Trot.

In our search for illustrations we were greatly helped by Harry Gilonis and Michael R. Leaman; the text profited from various suggestions and queries from Jonathan Burt and Martha Jay.

Photo Acknowledgements

The author and publishers wish to express their thanks to the following sources of illustrative material and/or permission to reproduce it. Locations, etc., of some items are also given below.

From Ulisse Aldrovandi, *De Animalibvs insectis libri septem cvm singvlorvm iconibvs ad viuum expressis...* (Bologna, 1638): p. 129; collection of the artist (Louise Bourgeois), courtesy Robert Miller Gallery, New York: p. 125; collection of the author: p. 134; photo David Beatty/Robert Harding/Rex Features: p. 6; Bibliothèque Centrale du Museum National d'Histoire Naturelle, Paris: p. 132; from John Blackwall, *A History of the Spiders of Great Britain and Ireland*, vol. II (London, 1864): p. 9; Bodleian Library, Oxford: p. 55; © Louise Bourgeois, DACS, London/VAGA, New York 2010: pp. 124, 125; British Museum, London (photo © Trustees of the British Museum): pp. 166, 168, 171; photos © Trustees of the British Museum: pp. 141, 145; from Johann Heinrich Campe, *Kinder Abeze* (Braunschweig, 1806): p. 74; photo Pete Carr/ www.petecarr.net: p. 159; from Jacob Cats, *EMBLEMATA, Amores Moresque, spectantia* . . . (Middleburg, 1618): p. 98; from Félicien Champsaur, *Masques Modernes* (Paris, 1889): p. 108; from Charles Clerk/Thomas Martyn, *ARANEI, or a Natural History of Spiders: INCLUDING the principal Parts of the Well known Work ENGLISH SPIDERS by Eleazar Albin, As also the Whole of the celebrated Publication ON SWEDISH SPIDERS By Charles Clerk; Revised, Enlarged and Designed anew By Thomas Martyn* (London, 1793): p. 86; from Johann Cuba, *Hortus Sanitatis* (Mainz, 1491): p. 128 (top); from R. A.

Ellis, *Im Spinnenland* (Stuttgart, 1913): p. 37; from books by J.-H. Fabre: pp. 33 – *La Vie des Araignées* ([?1928] Paris, 1949), 49 – *Souvenirs Entomologiques* (10 vols, Paris, 1879–1907); photo Donna Garde (http://www.texasento.net/Social_Spider.htm): p. 39; from Jeremias Gotthelf, *Die Schwarze Spinne von Gottheit* (Basel, 1937): p. 101; Graphisches Sammlung Albertina, Vienna: p. 110; Grünes Gewölbe, Dresden: p. 128 (foot); from Carl Wilhelm Hahn, *Die Arachniden. Getreu nach der Natur abgebildet und beschrieben*, vol. 1 (Nuremberg, 1831): pp. 23, 27, 29; Hamburger Kunsthalle: p. 142; photo Anneka James/ www.annekajames.co.uk/: p. 179; from C. L. Koch, *Die Arachniden. Getreu nach der Natur abgebildet und beschrieben*, vol. IX (Nuremberg, 1842): pp. 18, 19; photos Michael Leaman/Reaktion Books: pp. 13, 181; Library of Congress, Washington, DC: pp. 45 (Work Projects Administration Poster Collection), 99; photo Mike Maloney/Rex Features: p. 31; from Maria Sibylla Merian, *Metamorphosis Insectorum Surinamensium* (Amsterdam, 1705): p. 131; Museo del Prado, Madrid: p. 10; from 'Mynona' (Salomo Friedlaender), *Die Schöpfer* (Munich, 1920): p. 158; from *Narodnoje Delo* (1992): p. 150 (foot) photo Nature Picture Library/Rex Features: p. 24; photo Jon Nickles/US Fish and Wildlife Service: p. 22; from F. Petrarca, *Von der Artzney bayder Glück, des guten und Widerwärtigen* (Augsburg, 1532): p. 64; private collections: pp. 15, 136, 137 (top), 144; from *Punch* (1868): p. 153; from Paulus Aertsz. van Ravesteyn, *Sleutel-bloem vergadert... uit de schriften van Jacob Boehme* (Amsterdam, 1635): p. 78; photo Rex Features: p. 47; photo Roger-Viollet/Rex Features: p. 46; Royal Tombs of Sipán Museum, Lambayeque, Peru: p. 160; from Johann Jakob Scheuchzer, *Physica Sacra*, 4 vols (Augsburg and Ulm, 1731–5): p. 85; photo Joe Snyder/US Fish and Wildlife Service: p. 12; from *Sovjetskaja Moldavia* (1971): p. 150 (top); courtesy Spyder Europe AG: p. 14; from Jonathan Swift, *Voyages de Gulliver dans des contrées lointaines par Swift, édition illustrée par Grandville...* (Paris, 1838): p. 133; from *Ver Sacrum* (1898): p. 109; current whereabouts unknown: p. 182.

Index